All rights reserved. This book or any portion thereof
may not be reproduced or used in any manner
whatsoever without the express written permission of
the publisher except for the use of brief quotations in
a book review.

ISBN: 978-0-578-82068-2
Printed in the United States of America

THE SUPREME GUIDE TO AUTHENTIC SELF-CARE
& ELEVATION OF CONSCIOUSNESS.

DEDICATION

I dedicate this book to anyone led into my space during my own consciousness elevation journey. Your presence and energy, even if no longer in my space, caused a shift in my own process based on every choice I made in response to your influence on my reality, whether positive or negative. For all of it, I express gratitude, because all of you as a collective of experiences and messages to learn from have contributed to who and where I am today. I return this book to you, as a token of my appreciation, in hopes that reading it will help you to reunite with your higher self as well.

DISCLAIMER

The contents of this book were not written to serve as medical advice, but are intended for informational purposes only, and is not intended to replace or substitute any professional, financial, medical, legal or other advice. Please consult with your doctor about changes you will be making to your health and wellness, so that he/she can track along with any personalized blood tests, medication tweaking, chart documentation etc. needed. The contents of this book are also not intended to replace medical advice received by your healthcare professional team, inclusive of diagnoses and/or treatments received by your healthcare professional team. Never disregard or delay seeking professional medical advice or treatment from a healthcare professional because of the contents of this book.

By proceeding with this read, you are accepting and consenting to the above-mentioned details, inclusive of the fact that you expressly release the author of this book and her team from any and all liability concerning any treatment, action by, or effect on any persons following the information offered within this book. You should consult with an appropriately trained specialist for all concerns that require medical, legal, financial or other professional advice. Thank you.

CONTENTS

- **1** Prologue
- **6** Level One: You Always Have a Choice
- **12** Level Two: Mental Wellness
- **32** Level Three: Physical Wellness
- **59** Level Four: Spiritual Wellness
- **75** Level Five: Elevation of Consciousness
- **86** Level Six: Application of your Learnings
- **93** Acknowledgements
- **96** References

PROLOGUE

It was around 3 o'clock in the afternoon on a warm and sunny weekday. I stepped out of my parents 1983 Volvo sedan, smoothed down the skirt of my plaid Catholic school uniform dress, grabbed my back pack and marched through the driveway, completely unaware of the fact that I was on the verge of an experience that would stay with me for the remainder of my life. I kicked the gravel along the way just as I always did, creating patterns with my sneakers and launching the larger pebbles down the hill of the driveway like a bowling lane. I cut across the driveway into the grassy front yard of our condo, lost in a daydream yet still following close behind my father and younger sister.

My thoughts danced from what snack I'd have once I walked into our unit, to what game I would play outside in the yard, to acknowledgment of the giant yellow school bus that pulled up in front of our condo as it always did around this time to drop off the other children of our condo. I was fascinated by the yellow flashing lights on the bus that turned to red flashing lights, and I knew what came next... The little red stop sign that immediately popped out from the side. How cool. I watched the bus door slide open and saw a little brown boy step onto the bus steps and turn around, waving excitedly to the driver and the kids who remained on the bus. I was captivated by his smile. It was so big, so bright. It held my attention on him, preventing my focus and thoughts from moving on to anything else. I watched as the happy boy secured his backpack straps and proceeded down the bus stairs. His smile made me smile. I noticed that instead of stepping on the sidewalk and coming up the hill towards me, he turned in the opposite direction to walk across the front of the bus. "Oh," I thought, "he's not coming here. He must be going to visit a friend across the street or something."

I saw as the bus driver patiently waited for him to cross. As he made it to the solid yellow street lines that divided the two-lane street, his stride did not break, and neither did my gaze. I felt like I was walking with him. There was no need to look both ways. The small, red stop sign that popped out meant everyone had to stop for him, including the cars going in the opposite direction on the other side of the yellow lines. What I never fathomed was that even with the red stop sign, some drivers do not stop. The boy didn't seem to consider it either, as his first step from the yellow line was his last. He was suddenly struck by a white car that was going so extremely fast! It was as if the driver completely missed all speed limit signs, missed the giant yellow bus with flashing red lights, missed the bright red stop sign sticking out into their lane, and most importantly, missed a whole child in the middle of the street. The car struck him with such force that upon impact, his small body was flung into the air several feet like a rag doll, and I watched as his body did what looked like seven or eight flips mid-air before crashing back down onto the pavement. As his tiny body hit the pavement, the only way I could quantify the force of his landing was through the observation that upon impact, his backpack exploded. All contents of the backpack, I mean every single thing, splattered across the street.

Everything from that moment on seemed to happen like snapshots from a movie. I frantically tried to process the snapshots as quickly as they darted through my reality. The first snapshot was of the white car coming to a screeching halt several feet after the deadly impact. I processed that they were going THAT fast that it took them THAT long of smashing the breaks to get the car to stop.

The next snapshot was that of people emerging from various doors of the condo (including my mother), the houses around us, and homes across the street. I processed that they had all heard the impact and knew exactly what that sound meant. From my view, each adult was in a panicked state of shock. There was a moment of not knowing if the victim was one of their own. I felt it. I felt them holding their breaths. I felt the collective anxiety and fear as I watched their horrified faces. They came from everywhere, racing towards the bus, some in hair rollers, some in shower robes, some barefoot.

The next snapshot was of the man and woman who exited the white car, jogging down the street towards the school bus. I didn't know which one was the driver. They ran together, striding in unison, tears in their eyes. I processed that they were in shock too. That they were sorry. They didn't mean to do it.

The next snapshot included my own mother. My father ordered my sister and me to go inside with him. I moved slightly like I was following them and then stayed back. I made eye contact with my mom. I processed that in that moment, she knew I wasn't going to leave. I wasn't going to leave the boy. She proceeded to call 911. I had a moment where I thought I should be crying too, but I never cried. I thought I should be screaming too, but I never screamed. I thought I should be leaving too, like my sister and the other kids, or at least wanting to look away, but I never moved, not one inch. I was watching the boy. Something told me to stay for him, and I listened.

The next snapshot that came was of me observing one of the adults that came running out in the beginning. She was special. She was the one who made the realization that it was HER son that was hit. Her shrieks pierced my ears like sounds you'd hear coming from a haunted house. She fell on top of him and scooped him into her arms, sobbing and rocking. I processed that this was her baby, and that he was hurt REALLY bad. As I continued to watch, I saw the boy's body start shaking in his mother's arms, first like a winter shiver and then more violently and uncontrolled. I heard his mother scream, "He's cold! Someone get him a blanket!"

The next snapshot that came was of my mother emerging from our unit, holding MY baby blanket! The initial thought of "Hey! That's MY blanket!" was immediately replaced by a calm knowing that the boy needed it more than I did. As I watched my mom drape my blanket over his limp body, I strangely processed that he was not cold, but was leaving us. I had never experienced, studied, read about, learned about, or watched anything about death yet, but I had a strange knowing that he had died at that moment, under my blanket.

I wanted to do more to help the boy. I wished I could have saved him. Brought him back so that all of these adults would not be shouting and weeping. I wanted everyone to be happy and whole again. I was six years old.

When I first made the decision to go to medical school, I was ignorant of the magnitude of what God had in store for me. All I knew was that ever since I was six years old, I always had the nagging urge to help people feel better than how they currently felt. No more pain, no more imbalance. I wanted to spend my life making people feel less broken.

To my junior-high brain, that meant becoming a medical doctor, so I eagerly committed to that path. I can now say that receiving my MD was only the beginning, a stepping stone, a key to get me through the first of a series of doors to enable full alignment and execution of my life's purpose in this Earthly realm.

Now, having made my way through a few of those doors, my desire has expanded from merely "healing everyone" to EQUIPPING everyone with the tools, space, and consciousness elevation to activate healing THEMSELVES! I am clear that a significant portion of my purpose is to elevate God's people on all levels – mentally, physically, and spiritually.

I am obedient and aligning more and more with this purpose every day, and oh, it feels magical. Nearly dreamlike! I encourage you to consume this book with an open mind and an open heart in honor of my wish for you to one day experience the dreamlike magic of purpose alignment and consciousness elevation as well.

LEVEL 1

YOU ALWAYS HAVE A CHOICE

"At the end of the day, when everything is stripped away, at the core all we really get is time and choices. Be wise with both." – Dr. K.

THERE'S NO TIME TO WASTE!

knew it! I knew that the last thing I'd come up with while completing this book would be the title – and it was. I came up with all kinds of fancy titles – some very metaphysical-sounding and some just trendy catchphrases. I tucked them away, knowing that although I liked each of them, I didn't LOVE any one in particular. Then, they were out of sight and out of mind. That is, until one random, routine morning.

Opening the glass shower door to test the water temperature, I told myself that I would turn this shower into a cleansing meditation session, which wasn't uncommon for me. I selected my hemi-sync tune of choice on my cell phone and stepped into the shower. As the water draped my skin like a warm, silky blanket, I envisioned myself washing away negative energy and restoring love and light. I smiled in the enjoyment of my visualizations, and then, something happened. My visualizations of love and light were rudely interrupted by a stream of thoughts that intruded the seat of my consciousness, uninvited. They presented themselves to me in quick, short bursts of motion pictures. I saw myself aligning with my purpose. I saw myself doing things to make sure I was fully present in my self-care routine. I saw the aspects of my self-care routine that were not as strong as others or pushed to the back-burner for something else that I had deemed more important. I saw millions of other people - humanity itself - struggling to get by, merely surviving this thing we call life. People who didn't feel the luxury of positioning themselves to begin to execute a purpose. I saw all of us as a collective, professing things that we would "do later" or were "about to begin doing soon" to take better care of ourselves, but never get around to. Just as boldly as the snapshots bombarded their way into my thoughts, they vanished. Then, as I began to make sense of it all, I heard it. Soft like the faint melody of wind chimes in the distance, and gentle like birds chirping nature's symphony in the early morning, I heard it. It was a whisper, but extremely clear: "*No time to waste!*" I stepped out of the shower and typed the words into the Notes section of my iPhone.

ELEVATE WITH DR. K.

How would you feel if I told you that the revelations you'll receive while consuming this delicious content are guaranteed to help you elevate your consciousness if applied? Excited, perhaps, about the thought of meeting your higher self very soon? Nervous, perhaps, about the unknown and the changes that will undeniably occur through your transformation? Apprehensive, perhaps, about the potential work you may have to put in to achieve the results you want?

I want you to really replay the question in your mind and become present to the emotions that consume you. Whatever they may be, just know that they are perfectly fine. You are making the right decision to continue reading, no matter where you are in life and what you feel right now. In fact, the goal here is not to say that your current state – your current level of consciousness – is good or bad, right or wrong. It just is.

The power of this book is that it will meet you exactly where you are, no matter where that is at the moment you are reading it. Things will resonate with you to the capacity at which you are open, ready, and willing to receive them. In other words, each time you pick up this book, you may receive a different message from an excerpt you have already read at a previous time. That is perfectly fine and actually expected.

Now that you are fully aware of and okay with how you feel in this moment, become fully aware of and okay with your current level of consciousness (or lack thereof). Remember, whether you are at an elevated level of consciousness, or perhaps unconscious, it does not make you better or worse than the next person. It just is what it is, and the more transparent you are about exactly where you feel you fall on the consciousness spectrum, the more accurate the lens will be that you will wear as you read this book.

WHAT IS CONSCIOUSNESS?

It may help you to more quickly pinpoint where you fall on the consciousness spectrum if you had a better grasp of just what "being conscious" means to you. Many believe that to be conscious is to simply be aware. An awareness that spans beyond the scope of your environment and physical being. It's a more profound awareness of yourself holistically, starting with combining your mental, physical, and spiritual realms into one cognizant realization.

Others approach consciousness through developing a confident grounding and control over all aspects of self through perspective, thoughts, and actions. It entails the very reality you are experiencing and calling "life". Consciousness could be one of the greatest metrics existing to quantify your progress of personal transformation and development. Therefore, no matter where you fall on the consciousness spectrum, there is always room for growth and elevation! No human being can say they are finished elevating and have achieved full and total consciousness. In fact, part of the very nature of being human involves the element of imperfection and a lack of omniscience. Perfection, omniscience, omnipotence... Yeah, that would be God.

ARE YOU CONSCIOUSLY UNCONSCIOUS?

If you feel that you are on the lower end of the consciousness totem pole, or even unconscious, it's important to genuinely investigate the underlying cause of your position. This is important because it is the first step to becoming more conscious (if that is what you desire). In fact, many individuals are operating comfortably in a lower vibration and detachment from awareness. They are okay with being consciously unconscious. Again, this type of person is not evil or worse than the individual ready to seek enlightenment right now.

The key is to become present with whom you are. Understand the motivation and underlying cause behind you being in said space, and acknowledge whether or not you wish to remain there.

Typically, in determining whether or not you are consciously unconscious, it would help first to understand the three buckets that one could fall into regarding their unconsciousness. I like to refer to these as the trinity of unconsciousness.

BUCKET ONE: Laziness or Cowardice. You don't feel like being conscious or elevating your current level of consciousness (i.e. seems like it would be too hard, seems like it would be too much work, etc.) so you don't bother. You're too afraid of being conscious or elevating your consciousness (i.e. you're fearful of what it might expose, you're fearful of the unknowns this kind of transformation might bring, etc.).

BUCKET TWO: Ignorance or Unfamiliarity. You don't know how to be conscious or elevate your consciousness (i.e. you're just so overwhelmed with trying to figure out how to do it that you don't do it at all).

BUCKET THREE: Apathy or Indifference. You simply don't care to be conscious or elevate your consciousness (i.e. it's just not your thing, this is insignificant to you at this time, etc.) so you don't entertain it).

Do any of these resonate with you? Identifying which speaks to you the most (if any) holds significance because each anecdote is different. For instance, the anecdote to bucket one involves intentional sources of MOTIVATION, the anecdote to bucket two involves intentional sources of EDUCATION and the anecdote to bucket three involves intentional sources of INSPIRATION. All of which can be sourced by continuing through the remainder of this book!

Remember, if you identify yourself as an unconscious individual, with the underlying cause of your unconsciousness being ignorance, no worries! The information and enlightenment you'll receive by the time you complete this book will eliminate the ignorance because you will not be able to "un-discover" what you are about to discover about yourself. If you identify yourself as an unconscious individual, with the underlying cause of your unconsciousness being apathy or laziness, no worries! Continue to make your way through this book because at some point, your apathy or laziness will shift, and you will need the tools you are about to learn from this book to get to work. How am I so confident that you will eventually depart from the apathy and laziness buckets? Well, another attribute of being human involves the fact that we are basically wired to eventually desire change and elevation. Evolution is an integral part of us down to a cellular level. It's a part of our DNA configuration. So, although you may not desire elevation at this very moment, you will eventually some point in time. So, let's proceed with the initial phase of consciousness elevation: Comprehension and control of your mental realm!

LEVEL 2

MENTAL WELLNESS

*"Your mind can either serve you delightfully,
or govern you treacherously."* –Dr. K.

THE FACULTY OF CONSCIOUSNESS AND THOUGHT

I like to begin with comprehension and control of the mental realm because it seems that the other realms fall in line more effortlessly once mental wellness is enhanced. In other words, your other realms (i.e. your body, your spirit, your emotions, etc.) seem to simply follow the state of your mind.

When I speak of the state of the mind, or your mental wellness, it is not to be confused with mental "illness" or mental "disease." I love the description of the mind as being our faculty of consciousness and thought. In other words, with mental wellness, I am referring to the current quality of your thoughts, your words, your perspective, and your attitude. Are these things mostly positive or mostly negative? Are these aspects propelling you into inspiration and creation mode, or are they throwing you into fear and survival mode? Are they serving and fueling you, or are they mostly depleting and destroying you?

If your mental wellness is weak or destructive, you can easily manifest disease (physical realm), and even stagnancy or blockages executing your purpose (spiritual realm). On the other side of the same coin, if your mental wellness is stable or heightened, you can easily manifest an abundance in health, wealth, love, and self-awareness (or elevated consciousness). Let me share a few tokens within your mental realm to help get the ball rolling to amplify your mind's current state.

PERSPECTIVE

If a tree falls in a forest and no one is there, does it make a sound? The answer to this (which you'll uncover by the end of this section) has everything to do with perspective.

Perspective is what you create from the information and stimuli you are taking in with your senses and organizing with your mind. It's important to realize that at any given moment, two people sharing the same experience in the same location could be receiving completely different stimuli. Or, if they happen to have taken in similar stimuli, their brains may have filtered and organized them very differently in their minds. This is how you can have two eyewitnesses of the same event who express their accounts of what occurred with two different interpretations. The important message to gain from this is that most people are 100% convinced that their perception IS reality when, in fact, your perception is simply YOUR reality. Yes, you read correctly. There is life, and then there is YOUR perspective of it, which are two different experiences.

Evaluating and really sitting with your perspective is crucial if you want different or enhanced results in life. Your perspective gives rise to your thoughts and emotions. It is your thoughts and emotions that give rise to your actions. It is your actions that give rise to the results you are getting. Understanding the flow of these concepts is a key component to living a life you completely love effortlessly and powerfully.

Now, since your reality is simply a reflection of your mind (perspective), there are a few silver linings you need to know about:

1. If your reality is simply a reflection of your mind, and you don't like how your life/reality is going or looking right now, you have the power to alter it!
2. If your reality is simply a reflection of your mind, you have the power to manipulate how you experience it and even to create new and enhanced aspects of your reality in real time!
3. If your reality is simply a reflection of your mind, and your life/reality is looking a little gloomy right now (i.e. it seems like negative thing after negative thing keeps occurring), you have the power to shift the quality of circumstances you're involved in and begin attracting to yourself whenever you want!

Being able to tap into this power would require an understanding of your powers to create, to attract and to manifest. So, of course, I'll dive into these three areas shortly so you can begin applying them sooner than later. It is also key to comprehend the magnitude of influence behind taking the time to enhance your perspective. It is, at a very deep level, the underlying cause of the results you are getting in life right now, whether you love them or hate them. Remember the equation that it is your very perspective that fuels your thoughts and emotions; then it is your thoughts and emotions that fuel your actions. Your actions are yielding the results you are obtaining. If you love your life and the results you are getting, great! But for majority of readers of this book, they are experiencing results that they want to stop or change. So, you can dissect the equation backwards, altering things step by step, or you can take a deep plunge into the perspective immediately because you understand it to be the root of the equation. For instance, do you want different results? Great, just change your actions. Don't quite know how to change your actions? No worries. Just take a critical and authentic audit of your thoughts and emotions. Don't like the quality of those? It's ok. Just evaluate and begin to shift your perspective. Or, you can just go ahead and begin doing work on your perspective now, knowing that it will cause a shift in your reality down the line.

This being said, I'd love to leave you with some actionable takeaways that you can begin to implement today for immediate and noticeable shifts in your perspective.

1. (1) Stop expecting the worst from other people. If you constantly assume that everyone else is acting with negative intentions, your reality will reflect that. It's interesting how often we do this, despite knowing it is impossible to know the true reasoning behind another individual's actions. So,

overriding this automatic act and instead assuming the best out of a person in any given situation will begin to transform your perspective and thus your reality. Try it! The next time someone cuts you off in traffic, don't be so quick to anger, resorting to horn pressing and name calling. Assuming the best would look something like you considering that maybe the driver has a pregnant woman in the car who went into labor so he needed to cut across lanes to quickly get off at the next exit. Or, perhaps there's a sick child in the vehicle who needs to be rushed to the nearest emergency room. Then, become present to your new thoughts, emotions, and responses.

2. Stop yourself from dreading things. How many times has your mood sunken on a Sunday because thoughts flashed across your mind about having to get up and go to work the next morning? In this case, Sunday became a blur wasted on negative emotions connected to a dread of Monday. Some people even dread Sundays too because Monday is coming. Instead of dreading things like a particular day of the week, dive a little deeper. The day of the week is not the actual problem. The problem is the lens through which you SEE the day of the week. Your perspective has categorized Mondays as an unpleasant obstacle, which is not true. Monday is simply a day of the week. In fact, the more you can remove the filter of dread from smaller, day-to-day challenges like this, the easier it will become to do so with larger challenges you face in life.

3. Focus on the present moment. Are you spending so much time stuck in the past or preparing for the future, that the PRESENT moments are swiftly passing you by? Does time seem to be flying by for you (i.e. "I was just in high school and now I'm planning my 45th birthday party!", or the "what day is it today?" mentality)? As you make your way through your day, slow down time and get more involved in your own life by reminding yourself to be present in each moment. Cut off the robotic motions. Take note of the changes to your thoughts, your emotions and even your actions during the day. Pay attention to how much more fulfilling and satisfying the day feels.

4. Begin to differentiate between what is in your control and what is not. Many understand this concept best through The Serenity Prayer, where God is asked to grant us the serenity to accept the things we cannot change, the courage to change the things we can, and the wisdom to know the difference. When going through a tough circumstance, just take a moment to pull away from the situation and assess whether or not it is in your control. This helps to prevent you from giving a situation excessive power over you, and from allowing the situation to consume you. There's no use deliberating when it was never in your control to begin with. For instance, if your entire division at work gets laid off, you can opt to sit and brood in this new reality and fall into a depression from the anxiety of your circumstances. Or, you can choose to accept the circumstance for what it is and what it is not, acknowledging what is out of

your control (it just is what it is). Then you can transition into your next step(s) with power to produce novel and productive results!

So, if a tree falls in a forest and no one is there, does it make a sound? After reflecting on all you have just read, what are your thoughts on the answer now? Well, consider that the answer is no. If a tree falls in a forest and no one is there, no it does not make a sound. Why not, you ask? Well, because sound results from your sensory perception. Now you see that we live in a completely subjective reality. Choices we make and actions we take based on the stimuli we have gathered with our senses and assessed with our brains all ban together to augment our perspective (aka our reality) which (again) you always have the power to alter!

CREATION

One of the most powerful gifts that we have been blessed with is an innate ability to create within our own lives. Creation of new circumstances, enhanced relationships, financial abundance, elevated health, renewed self, etc. through practice of the useful concepts known as attraction and manifestation. We will cover both in more detail shortly.

When tapping into your power to create, it is first imperative that you understand the authority behind your words. Words are very powerful creators of reality. In fact, without words, it's extremely difficult for a thought to become a reality. So, the next obvious realization is that we should strive to only pick the VERY BEST words in order to create your VERY BEST reality. This is where the statement "speaking things into existence" comes from. In fact, countless historical and religious texts reference the power and influence that our words embody. For instance, Proverbs 18:21 mentions, "The tongue has the power of life and death, and those who love it will eat its fruit."

We also see in the first page of the Book of Genesis, in the introduction to the creation story, that everything began by word alone; and that THIS word was backed by the power and the authority of God because the word itself WAS God.

Why do our words hold so much power? Well, I'm glad you asked! Consider the fact that it is your words that provide a bold affirmation of your inner most thoughts. Your words are a confirmation to the world of how you see others, your life, and yourself. Have you ever caught yourself saying out loud that you're not smart enough to do something or not good enough to accomplish something? You need to be careful with your choice of words and how they are affecting your very state of consciousness.

Try it right now! Instead of tearing yourself down with destructive language of what you cannot do and who you cannot be, shift the focus to what you CAN do and who you actually ARE. In this very moment, go ahead and recreate yourself. Affirm who you are with two of the most powerful words in terms of creation of your reality: "I AM."

Rather than ACTING a certain way, there is power in BEING a certain way. So, go ahead and recreate yourself with at least two new ways of being. Instead of trying to love everyone, just BE love. Instead of trying to make it through every rough situation that hits you, just BE resilience. Say to yourself out loud, "I am love. I am resilience." Whichever I am's you choose for yourself in this moment, profess them out loud and begin to align your perspective, thoughts, emotions, and actions with those words. For instance, if I am love, then all my thoughts, emotions and actions need to come from a place of love. If someone cuts me off in line, my reaction will come from a place of love. If someone tries to say something to rub me the wrong way at work, my response will come from a place of love. Just take this one day at a time, knowing that each day and each moment, you are always free to recreate yourself.

The key is maintaining the alignment with who you have recreated yourself to be. Remember who you are.

ATTRACTION

Before we start down the road of attraction, it is important to remember that life is not happening TO you. Rather, you are CREATING and ATTRACTING it as you go. When it comes to the Law of Attraction, believing it to be true or not doesn't change anything. It's a simple universal principle that is definitely occurring, much like the Law of Gravity. Whether you believe gravity is real or not, you are still subjected to it because gravity is an unchanging law of our universe. However, believing in the power of attraction and getting in tune with it allows you to better position yourself be in control of your reality. So, your very awareness of the Law of Attraction can completely transform your entire life.

When considering the Law of Attraction, it's important to take note of three things:

1. Like attracts like, and whether you realize it or not, you are responsible for bringing both positive and negative influences into your life. Whether you are doing it knowingly or unknowingly, every second of your existence, you are acting as a human magnet sending out your thoughts and emotions and then attracting back more of what you have sent out.
2. Where you place your focus can have a significant impact on what happens to you. If you spend your days wallowing in regrets about the past or fears of the future, you'll likely see more negativity appearing, but if you look for the silver lining in every experience then you'll soon start to see more positivity surrounding you.
3. The foundation of the Law of Attraction is to believe that it works. Then, the possibilities for attraction are only limited by your own imagination. How incredible is that!

In order to begin effectively attracting what you want into your life, you must take some quiet time with yourself to pinpoint exactly where your life is now and where you want it to be. When you understand that ANYTHING is possible, you eliminate the space for limiting beliefs, fear, doubt, and worry. In fact, worry is simply placing your thoughts, focus, and energy into something that you do NOT want to happen. So, because you create or attract more of what you are focusing on, worrying causes you to unintentionally create more of what you do not want. It's almost like starting a garden, and instead of planting the seed, watering it, and watching it grow, you dig the seed up every day to see what the seed is doing, thus stunting its progress.

When it comes to attracting, here are some tools to guide you on how to do it powerfully and effectively:

1. Now that you know that rather than ACTING a certain way, there is power in BEING a certain way, you can tap into a powerful way of being that unlocks highly abundant versions of attracting – GRATITUDE! Expressing gratitude is the key to setting yourself up for bigger and better things. Gratitude places you in the right mindset to receive them. Expect that God will be more likely to bless you if you are grateful for what has already been provided to you. In fact, being in a space of gratitude, elevates your consciousness; it immediately increases your vibrational frequency. Gratitude is a clear demonstration of not only appreciation of what you have and the availability to receive more, but also a TRUSTING in the process that more is coming.
2. Be able to vividly visualize in detail what it is that you wish to attract. Imagine what this new thing looks like, smells like, sounds like, feels like, etc. How do you feel once this new thing is in your life? Where do you feel it in your body? Does it make your toes tingle or make your heart flutter? Does your pulse race or do you feel a wave of calm? Make it real in your mind, and everything else follows. Don't just focus on receiving this

new thing; think of your life after receiving it too. Imagine how it will change your entire world.

3. No imposter syndrome allowed. Simply put, if you do not believe you deserve what you are seeking, you will not get it. Those deep, subconscious fears and doubts send conflicting messages that are just as loud and clear. Know that if part of you feels as though you do not deserve what you're seeking, then that part of you is competing with (and possibly intercepting!) your desires.

4. Whatever you direct and focus your energy on is what you will attract. This is especially key in language. For instance, every October I get invited to speak at various galas and conferences on breast cancer awareness. I always accept the invitation, with the condition the I do not have to speak on breast cancer awareness, because that would be me only directing and focusing my energy on the cancer. Which, by design, will only cause an attraction of more cancer. Instead, I let them know that I will be speaking on wellness awareness and ways you can enhance your lifestyle, mindset and spiritual hygiene to prevent having to deal with cancer at all in the first place. You see, through language, I have effortlessly shifted the focus to what I would love to attract more of.

Another great way of affirming what you would like to attract, so that your energy is always focused on it, is through the creation of a vision board. This is not just a cliché project to label as busy work. The very act of spending time finding images and words and attaching them to a board is a personal commitment to your desires. It helps you clarify what you really want, visualize it and put energy toward making it real. Then, each time you look at the board, the images serve as a great reminder and affirmation of your desires. This sort of repetition will lead you down the path of successful attracting!

MANIFESTATION

As you are powerfully attracting all sorts of goodness into your life, you can accelerate your progress by manifestation. How is manifesting different from attracting? Well, I'm so glad you asked! Some look at manifestation as the active component, while attraction is more of a passive pull of energy. In other words, manifestation involves YOU creating from your thoughts; attraction involves like attracting like. Through the Law of Attraction, you are attracting (more of) something that already exists. Manifestation is attributing the power of creating something that does not yet exist in your reality.

I have a very simple equation for efficiently manifesting to help you understand and apply it. Here it is: **I + M = R**

The "I" stands for the very bold and specific "intention" you desire and set for yourself to manifest. The "R" stands for the new "reality" you manifest. The "M" stands for "method(s)" you will utilize to get from point A (of not having what you desire) to point B (having manifested what you desire).

The first key to this equation working for you is remembering that the "I" must be bold and very specific. So, if it sounds like a wish, (i.e. "I would like to have..." or "It would be nice to have..."), that's not strong enough. The intention must be professed as if it is already happening or already in existence. For example, a solid intention is, "I will fly into Nigeria for a 2-week sabbatical by July 20th." This is bold because I did not say that I *would like to* go to Nigeria or *wish I could* go to Nigeria. Notice that it was specific. I did not say that I am going to Nigeria "soon" or "at some point in time in the future". The more specific and bolder, the better your chances of manifesting. Furthermore, as you are stating your intention, always focus on what you want rather than what you do NOT want. Remember the Law of Attraction here, what you continue to place focus on is what you will continue to attract. Language is everything in this case. For instance, rather than setting the intention to get rid of your high blood pressure, you set the intention to be whole and well. This shifts the focus from the high blood pressure to being whole and well, which cannot include having high blood pressure or any other health compromise for that matter.

The second key to this equation working for you holds a pivotal realization. The "M" is the point where the majority of people get stuck. For those who claim they cannot manifest or that manifestation does not work for them, the obstacle is usually regarding their actual methods. For some, their "I" was never clear or bold enough; yet for most, they get lost in the methods accompanying their intention. For instance, regarding the earlier example about going to Nigeria, some methods include: money, the ability to take time off from work (PTO hours), a plane ticket, etc. How many times have you desired something and even begun planning for it, only to not follow through because you don't feel you have enough money, or you don't feel you have enough time, or you don't feel you have enough resources, or you don't feel you have enough knowledge, or enough talent, and on and on? That's what getting stuck at the "M" looks like. However, the most empowering part of this equation (and of manifesting period) is true understanding that the "M" is the least important part of the equation. For the sake of illustration, let's just pretend that it doesn't exist at all. Now, look at the equation. When you remove the "M," notice that the equation now reads: **I = R**!

This exemplifies the astonishing revelation that your powerful and bold intention is already reality if you just continue to focus on IT (rather than the M)! It's all in your perception, and when you shift your perspective to operate from the fact that what you are manifesting is already real, you begin to align yourself with that fact. Here is another example: If your intention is that of improved health and wellness, then aligning yourself with this outcome as if it is already in existence would look like doing what healthy and well people do – going to bed and rising when healthy and well people would go to bed and rise, hanging out where healthy and well people would go, eating what healthy and well people would eat, drinking what healthy and well people would drink, setting up your daily itinerary to reflect a healthy and well person, etc. By doing so, there is no need to worry about or get stuck in the methods of *how to* become healthy and well. You have already aligned with it to the point that people on the outside looking in can't tell the difference. People begin to wonder and whisper among themselves about how they THOUGHT you had such and such diagnosis, but now they are not sure. Or how you don't LOOK like a person carrying the diagnosis that they THOUGHT you had. Your alignment becoming seamless is your "I" becoming your "R" without you ever even worrying about the "M" enough to get lost in it! It also doesn't end there. Your seamless alignment, causing people to believe that your intention is already a reality, also extends to yourself. Yes, you can cause your own subconscious mind to believe that your intention is already a reality! Notice how all of this proceeded from you shifting your focus from the method(s) to the intention.

Place all of your focus, energy, alignment, etc. on your bold and specific intention and let the manifesting begin!

Now, I know what you're thinking: How do I ensure that I am properly placing all of my focus and energy on my bold and specific intention? How do I know I'm genuinely aligning myself with the intention as if it already exists? Great questions! Let's dive deeper into alignment with your intention. Deep and authentic alignment with your intention requires the creation of my Manifestation Map! Through my years of working with people and coaching them through the art of manifesting, I was able to land on a tried-and-true method for ensuring that you manifest what you want in your desired time frame. I will now teach you the art of creating and adhering to the Manifestation Map, using my rules of three. *Side note for those wondering why three is the magic number, three is my favorite completion number and involved in many aspects of my life. So I was led to incorporate that in my creation of the Manifestation Map.* Your Manifestation Map will look like a cake with, yes you guessed it, THREE layers. We begin with the top layer and work our way down by asking one question, "How?" Each time you come up with a component of your Manifestation Map, the subsequent piece is generated by asking yourself that simple question, yes you guessed it again, THREE times. Your Manifestation Map will end up looking like this:

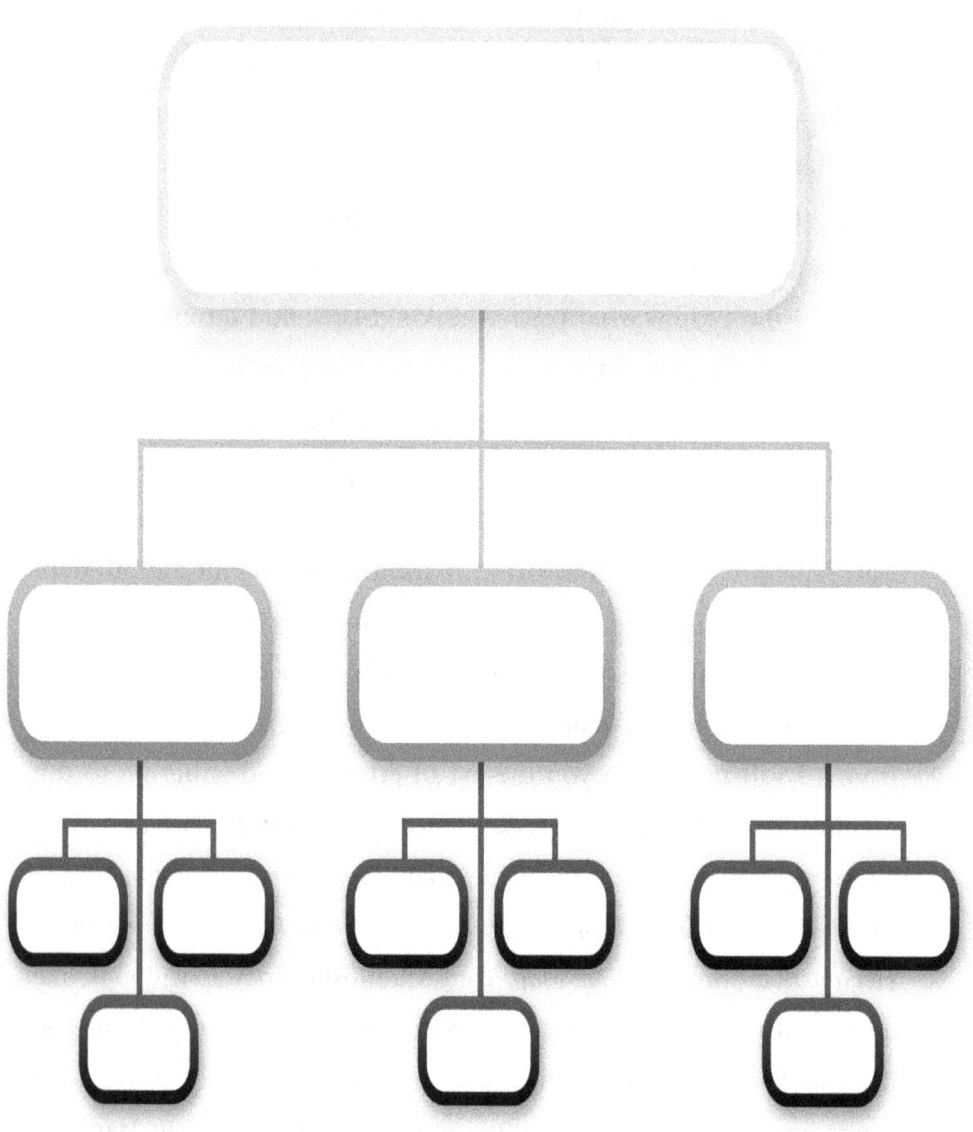

The largest, top layer of your Manifestation Map is where you will write your powerful intention. Remember to write it as if it is already in existence. Then have it be as specific as possible (i.e. include a manifestation date). Then, you ask yourself the magic question, "How?" How will you ensure that the top layer (your intention) comes to fruition?

Remember, the magic number three here. Come up with three ways you will ensure that the top layer manifests and note them in the three boxes below it. Also add dates to make the items more specific. For instance, continuing with the example above, the first box for me (in the second layer/tier) could be "I will book my ticket by March 1st. Next to it, the second box could be "I will come up with the exact 14 days that I can be in Nigeria, by February 1st. Then the third box could say "I will pull in an accountability partner (insert name here) by tomorrow, to help me ensure that I adhere to my Manifestation Map".

Once complete, you can move down to the third and final layer. Let's begin with the first box ("I will book my ticket by March 1st"). Remember, now you ask yourself the magic question, "How?" to begin filling in the three subsequent boxes in the final/third layer. So, how will I ensure that I book my ticket by March 1st? The first box below it could say "I will open up next Friday to work (I'm normally closed on Fridays), and devote all proceeds that day towards financing the trip so money is not a delaying factor." The second box could be "I will set an alarm on my phone to go off three days prior to March 1st as a 72-hour alert/call to action". The third box could be "One week prior to March 1st, I will reach out to a travel agent to learn what my travel options are."

Let's move onto the second box of the second tier ("I will come up with the exact 14 days that I can be in Nigeria, by February 1st"). Now, you ask yourself the magic question again, "How?" to take steps for filling in the 3 boxes. How will I ensure that I will come up with the exact 14 days that I can be in Nigeria? The first box could be "I will go into my personal schedule today and move things around so that I have a solid 14-day period free of obligations." The second box could be "I will go into my work schedule tomorrow and block myself as being 'out of office' for 14 days so nothing new gets scheduled." The third box could be "I will take tomorrow to also secure additional support around childcare for the 14-day period."

Finally, you can now move on to the third box of the second tier ("I will pull in an accountability partner [insert name here] by tomorrow to help me ensure that I adhere to my Manifestation Map"). You ask yourself the magic question, "How?" How will I ensure that I will secure said individual as an accountability partner? The first box could be "set a couple hours aside after dinner tonight to call (name) and make the request." The second box could be "During the conversation, I will share the details of my entire Manifestation Map." Doing this helps your accountability partner empathize with the passion and desire you have to manifest this intention. The third box could be "During the conversation, I will make the level of involvement of my accountability partner clear." For instance, sharing the specifics tasks I will need him/her to complete and the specific reminders I will need him/her to provide for me."

Through the very act of filling in your manifestation map, you are determinedly FOCUSING on your intention. Through the very act of hitting your manifestation map deadlines, you are powerfully ALIGNING your intention. This is you not getting stuck at the "M" of the equation. This is you being an unstoppable manifester of whatever it is that you want, at any point in time, to begin to construct the reality of your dreams.

LEVEL 3

PHYSICAL WELLNESS

"The healthier your body is, the easier it is for you to manifest what you want in this reality. Taking care of your body is a high-level expression of gratitude to God." –Dr. K.

THE PHYSICAL AND MORTAL ASPECT OF A PERSON

For a moment, think of your physical body in the way that you think of a rental car. You go get a loaner to drive out of town with the understanding that although you are driving it, putting gas in it, and responsible for its wellbeing, it is not yours. It does not belong to you. From the outside, people may be convinced that you are the owner; but YOU know that you are not the owner and the OWNER knows you are not the owner, and that is really all that matters. You have a contract that you've probably slipped into the glove compartment serving as a written reminder of this fact, including when exactly you were given the vehicle and when you are required to return it. Additionally, there are rules (spoken and unspoken) to follow upon return of the vehicle. Personally, I clean out the car, fill the gas tank, and make sure the car is as close as possible to the same condition it was given to me in.

Now, consider your physical body. To enter this Earthly realm, you were gifted with an Earthly body that was shaped and created just for you. You are responsible for its general wellbeing and the knowing that, at the end of the day, it is not yours. It does not belong to you.

From the outside, people may be convinced that you are the owner; but YOU know that you are not the owner and the OWNER knows you are not the owner, and that's all that matters. Although our physical bodies do not come with a written contract that you can save somewhere the rules still apply. The information has been documented in several places, historical texts, religious texts, spiritual texts and, most importantly, it has been etched in your soul.

Furthermore, although we are not afforded the ability of knowing our "return date" ahead of time, this detail should actually be the motivational drive to keep your vessel impeccable at all times, ensuring you are always prepared and not taken by surprise when your "return date" finally comes. Our card can be pulled any day, any time; and because we have no idea of when that moment is, you must treat each day like it could be the one. Remember, I clean out the car, fill the gas tank, and make sure that it is as close as possible to the same condition that it was in when it was initially given to me. Most people who do the same probably do so the day the vehicle is due back. However, when considering the physical body and the fact that we don't KNOW the return day, procrastination NEVER works in our favor. Your maintenance work has to be done regularly. Your refueling has to be done regularly. Your cleansing and detoxing has to be done regularly. The determination to have your body look, function, and serve you as close to the way it did when you were young should be fervent.

One aspect of wellness that is highlighted often in our society is disease. Do we want to continue this global focus on disease, only to perpetuate more of it? Let's, instead, reframe our thinking for a moment from disease reversal and disease prevention to wellness awareness and wellness maintenance. Imagine where we would be in society if instead of funneling billions of dollars towards disease or disorder campaigns like cancer awareness, AIDS awareness, autism awareness, etc., we shifted as a collective towards the massive funding of wellness awareness campaigns, 5K races, wellness programs, etc.! Remember, it is through the acknowledgement and enhancement of your current state of wellness that you generate an elevated expression of alignment and an authentic expression of love and gratitude onto God.

DON'T WAIT FOR THE DIAGNOSIS

As you make your way along the physical aspect of your wellness journey, it's important to remind yourself that you were created to fulfill a greater agenda than being born, working, and dying. That life is farthest from the type of life we were created to experience during our short time here. When you arrive at the portion of the book where I go into purpose discovery and alignment, it would be very discouraging if after all the work you put into discovering it, you could not execute that purpose because of an imbalance in your physical realm that is holding you back. This imbalance can manifest in many ways, including full-blown disease(s), exhaustion, excess weight, physical pain, or lack of motivation to do anything all.

I invite you to consider the fact that by the time you DO receive a diagnosis, you have done much more damage to your body than you think. Our bodies were ingeniously designed with impeccable precision and impressive processes to support and heal itself. God created many fail-safe designs within the human body. For instance, if one system gets chronically compromised or even fails, another system kicks in to compensate for it to reduce the potential of harm to you. If that system becomes compromised or fails then (again) another immediately kicks to keep things flowing as adequately as possible, and so on and so forth. It's a system that supports your very survival. The back-ups may not work as well as the system originally designed to take on that physiological responsibility, but it will do what it needs to do to help chip in to keep you alive. Once you have received a medical diagnosis it is highly likely that you have blown through at least one or more of the fail-safe designs. Not listening to or giving attention to your body's cues, a lack of proactivity with your own body, and a lack of oneness with your own body interrupts this divine system. It's necessary to realize this because we are created in God's image and likeness, so your body was created to perform optimally, not to suffer. Then you are prescribed a pill or treatment constructed to address the imbalance that has been brewing over time.

We must begin to take charge of our physical wellness, not only because of the obvious result of feeling better, but also because it aligns you with our unique reason for being created. Doing so means we show up as our best selves physically to impact humanity! Don't wait for a medical professional to serve you with a diagnosis (or for some, ANOTHER diagnosis) before you decide it's time to pull the blindfold from your eyes. Take action now! Begin to take better care of your body today! Who could not use increased energy levels and a better ability to accomplish daily goals? Who would not want an enhanced ability to concentrate on and blow through any given task? Physical imbalance tends to bleed into other aspects of your life, thus taking a toll on your overall happiness and ability to live a fulfilled life.

I hear you asking, "But where do I even begin?" I'm glad you asked! We ALL can begin in the area of the physical realm that we have so much control over and use on a daily basis to cause or prevent disease – the lifestyle!

THE FIVE PILLARS OF YOUR LIFESTYLE

Epigenetics is the study of cellular and physiological traits, or the external and environmental factors, that turn our genes on and off, and in turn, define how our cells read those genes. It works to see the true potential of the human mind, and the cells in our body (1). Through my years of studying and enhancing (or hacking) lifestyles to impact physical wellness in a fast and positive way, I concluded on five areas of the physical realm that I consider to be inclusive of the dynamic composition that I call *lifestyle*. I have found that when these five pillars are balanced and elevated, it is extremely difficult to manifest or even maintain anything in the human body that does not serve your physically wellness in a constructive way. This is for the people who feel that they are doomed to have something undesirable in their physical realm because family members have/had it. This is for the people who have been told that what they are currently experiencing will be with them (and in this severity) for the rest of their lives. This is for the people who feel that nothing is wrong, but they want to keep things that way. This is for the people who seek empowerment in knowing that they DO have control over their physical realm and there ARE things that can be done regularly so that life as they know it as it pertains to their physical realm is not just "happening TO them." Anyone, any ethnicity, any gender, any age can elevate these pillars and thus elevate this realm of wellness. The five pillars of your lifestyle include: diet, stress, rest, physical activity, and toxin exposure.

DIET

This seems to be the most important aspect of the lifestyle to people because it definitely gets the biggest spotlight. The truth is that all five pillars are equally important, and when people play favoritism with the pillars, the result is an imbalanced lifestyle where you are still susceptible to the unfavorable diseases that plague the physical realm. This is why there are some people who eat extremely clean but still battle with disease. No one pillar can carry you all by itself.

It is vital to understand that your diet represents all things consumed by the human body, not just food. You must take into account all beverages consumed, all supplements consumed, all things consumed aromatically, all things absorbed through the hair, skin, nails, etc. Now, please take a quick moment to re-examine your diet, and consider how you would rate the quality of your diet.

When it comes to your way of eating, before picking which trending diet of the month you are going to sign yourself up for, it's important to first consider what your relationship with food is. Many of us have a poor and even unhealthy relationship with food and that's where the issues begin. We view eating as an activity of indulgence, something to make us happy, something to make us feel better. There is nothing wrong with incorporating food in moments of celebration or within the communion of friends/family. The problem is the pleasure-seeking box we tend to put food into, which changes its dynamic. It becomes more of an addictive drug than as the literal energy our bodies need to function optimally. Let's reframe our thinking to view food as fuel. Each time you consume anything, you should ask yourself if your body is being fueled in a way that will enable it to perform better and to better serve you (or not).

How would you know, you ask? Well, this is where we consider the very sustenance of the fuel itself – the nutrients. Nutrients are the things your body extracts from each item you eat (i.e. vitamins, minerals, fats, carbohydrates, proteins, water, fiber, etc.). Your cells do not care how beautiful the cake looked, how moist the muffin was in your mouth, or how refreshing the can of soda was. The digestion process, in a nutshell, involves the breakdown of your food where nutrients can be extracted and reabsorbed as easily as possible, concluded by the disposal of what remains as waste. You can look at nutrients as the driving force of your cellular processes; the dialect or language that your cells use to speak to one another; the currency of communication exchange between organs and organ systems at large. Every time you consume something, you want to look at the quality of your fuel. Think of yourself as a luxury vehicle and visualize the nature of the fuel you have been replenishing with lately. Have you been fueling with anything less than premium oil?

The other key thing to do here is to begin shifting your mindset to use your food as medicine. Our home, the Earth, was blessed with an abundance of food groups and herbs throughout nature that were created for nourishment and to foster healing and general wellness. When you combine viewing your food as premium-grade fuel with using your food to promote internal balance, natural healing, and optimization of physiological systems, you now have a head start on reinforcing the relationship between you and your food.

Within the United States (and many other countries who have now adopted our first-world lifestyle tendencies), we need to pause and look at what is hurting and killing us the most so that we can address them (and their underlying causes) head on. What is HURTING us the most in the United States is that we have managed to construct the alarming statistic of being the most overfed, yet most undernourished people of the world. This disturbing detail is one of the most prominent underlying causes of what is KILLING us the most – cardiovascular disease – year after year. In fact, if you were sitting in a group of four right now reading this book together, one of you (statistically speaking) would die from some form of cardiovascular disease. According to the Centers for Disease Control and Prevention, *"One person dies every 37 seconds in the United States from cardiovascular disease...[and]...about 647,000 Americans die from heart disease each year..."*. (2)

When I encounter someone with any variation of heart disease, my mind immediately resorts to pulling back the onion layers, as it were, to uncover the root causes. My mind dances around the build-up of chronic inflammation and mucous in the body, but what would be the root cause of THAT? My mind then hones in on a breach somewhere in the lifestyle. There is an imbalance somewhere in the five pillars, but what would be the root cause of THAT? Then, it hits me. As my mind sits with an underlying cause, I am forced to acknowledge that the true root cause of death in the United States, one that will never be displayed on a medical website because there is no lab test or clinical way to "confirm" it, is IGNORANCE.

How can we shift this diet pillar? I'm glad you asked! Because our bodies are on this persistent quest for nutrients from all that we consume, let's give it what it needs! This requires you to consume more nutrient-dense foods and beverages. Alter your meal's portion-sizes to include items with the most nutrients making up the majority or at least 50% of your plate. You can also make sure your meal comprises as many nutrients as possible by eating as colorfully as possible. Every food color represents a different nutrient, so eating a rainbow of colors on each plate will help with giving you a variety of nutrients. Is there a food color you now notice you do not consume regularly that you can begin incorporating? As you think about this, do not forget the black foods, which are extremely rich in antioxidants and disease-fighting power. You can also incorporate supplements under the guidance of a healthcare professional who is proficient in supplement therapy and nutrient acquisition to ensure your body is getting optimal nutrient consumption, and correct any nutrient imbalances you may already have.

Chronic inflammation is an underlying cause of what is statistically supposed to pre-maturely claim most of our lives. So, always ask yourself, of the food items you are torn between eating, which are the most anti-inflammatory? In other words, which food item, which meal, which beverage, which diet, etc. will prevent or reduce the chronic inflammation in my body the most? A sobering reality is that nearly half of the calories consumed in this country now come from nutritionally depleted foods. Therefore, it's not only about facing the obesity epidemic, but also facing the fact that there are diseases being flipped on internally that you were never intended to exist in the first place. It would also behoove you to eliminate those food items/groups that negatively impact the body, such as processed foods, inorganic produce, and genetically modified organisms (GMOs). Stay away from boxed, bagged, and canned foods, items that come with a long list of unnatural ingredients, and instead focus more on cleaner eating comprised of mostly plant-based foods or whole foods (i.e. vegetables, fruits, legumes, beans, lentils, nuts, seeds, etc.).

Finally, please do not forget to incorporate what I feel is the most important nutrient of all – water! Water is your body's principal chemical component, and EVERY physiological system depends on it to function optimally, as we are ourselves roughly 70%-80% water! Daily hydration is important because you actually lose water every moment (i.e. via perspiration, urination, bowel movements, respiration, certain medical conditions, etc.). Appropriate daily hydration to replenish the loss and maintain the reserves for the average individual leading a mild to moderately active lifestyle is going to be consumption of about half of your body weight in ounces of water daily. For instance, a 200-pound individual should be aiming for about 100 ounces of water daily. Of course, there are exceptions to this. If you move to a hotter climate or increase your current level of physical activity, which in turn increases your perspiration rate, you will need to consume more water daily. If you are sick (i.e. fever, vomiting, diarrhea, etc.) or nursing, causing more rapid fluid loss, then you will need a higher daily water intake. If you have a medical condition (i.e. heart disease/failure, kidney disease/failure, etc.) where you may be on a fluid restriction and/or dealing with fluid imbalance in the body you should consult with your doctor to gain clarity around what your maximum daily water intake should be.

As you read this book, the water in your body is currently doing countless things for you. It is keeping your mucosal membranes moist, it is enabling cellular growth, reproduction and survival, it is flushing your system of waste, it is lubricating your joints, it is needed by your brain to manufacture hormones and neurotransmitters, it is regulating your body temperature, it is acting as a shock absorber for your brain and spinal cord, and it is assisting in the delivery of oxygen throughout your body, in addition to so many other performances. This is why every system needs it, in considerable amounts, to collectively ensure that you are functioning the way you need to on a regular basis.

When it comes to the consumption of water, it's important to realize that if the equation regarding how much water to consume daily seemed like a massive amount, then perhaps you join the tens of thousands of people who have been walking around under hydrated for the majority of their lives.

Another way you can gauge how under hydrated you are is by assessing the toilet bowl after urinating. You want your urine to be as odorless and as colorless as possible. You have to remember the toilet bowl is already filled with water, so the color of your urine that you see is actually a diluted version of what the color actually is. Being under hydrated may not necessarily land you in the hospital as often as dehydration could, but it is still harmful to your health because the functionality of systems within your body will be compromised. It's almost as if your cellular processes are being dumbed down to function as best they can.

When it comes to diet, our perspectives must shift. Instead of ignoring or trying to make sense of food ingredients that do not make sense in the first place, adjust your mindset to accept that if you cannot pronounce it then you probably should not be eating it. Also, instead of joining the narrative around how expensive organic food is, develop a new one that calls out how cheap processed food is. Start wondering about what you see. If there is a section of the store that is the "more natural" or the "more health-conscious" section, then what is that really saying about the rest of the store? Start to research things that do not add up. If the chemicals in pesticides are designed to kill insects, small bugs, bacteria, fungus and even plant diseases, and if the chemicals in herbicides are designed to kill undesirable weeds, then what good could it possibly be doing to us who then eat those foods covered in these chemicals? Thoughts like these should begin to dance across your mind as you elevate within this pillar of your lifestyle. The focus should be on what you are incorporating to elevate as opposed to what you must "deprive yourself of." Focusing on what you are adding and shifting creates a mindset of abundance rather than one of deprivation or scarcity. It's easier to augment this pillar where your body tells you what no longer serves it. Then, you simply listen and comply. Align with your physical realm, pay attention to your body, honor your body, and be obedient to its communications so your overall wellness flow becomes more effortless.

STRESS MANAGEMENT

When it comes to stress, our perspectives must shift. Please understand that stress is a PROCESS/RESPONSE (not a feeling) and is truly a SILENT destroyer and often times killer of lives. This form of stress is what I refer to as CHRONIC stress, because a little bit of stress is actually needed for our survival as a species. The stress response itself is not problematic and was, in fact, designed to move us quickly out of harm's way could thrive and evolve. The problem arises when the stress is on-going or happening repetitively. THIS is chronic stress.

The way our stress response was designed is highly intricate when you really understand what's going on. The adrenal glands – the two tiny glands that sit on top of either kidney – are the key players in this entire response. They are the ones responsible for pushing out all the chemicals, hormones, etc. needed for you to initiate the "fight, flight, or freeze" responses to a stressor/perceived threat. This innate response system has been with us since the beginning of time, well before our current level of civilization. So, imagine how we were living before these times. This response was designed to move you out of harm's way if you were, for example, confronted by a wild animal (let's use a saber-toothed tiger for illustration purposes). So, you suddenly find yourself in front of this intimidating beast that could end your life. Your body immediately engages the stress response system to save you. You are flooded with the chemicals and hormones that begin to make changes in your physiology. Organ systems instantly reprioritize themselves because energy must be conserved and redirected to the parts of your body that need it most. Your body instinctively knows it can't waste a single ounce of energy doing something that does not contribute towards survival! As the saber-toothed tiger draws closer and closer to you, your body realizes this is a moment where you will have to fight the tiger or run from the tiger (and hopefully not fall into the third "freeze" option which was newly added to the "fight or flight" model after seeing a pattern of this response).

This is not the time to for planning or thinking. You need to ACT! Therefore, your cognitive functioning will be lessened because it's not a priority. Imagine your last major stress episode. Did you experience any brain fog, difficulty focusing, problems concentrating, weakened memory, or an overall feeling of being overwhelm and lost? This happened by design.

As the saber-toothed tiger draws closer to you, your body realizes this is not a good time to sit down and eat a sandwich or even have an appetite at all. Therefore, your digestive functioning will be lessened because it, too, is not a priority. Think again back to your last major stress episode. Did you experience upset stomach, diarrhea, constipation, nausea, vomiting, acid reflux, indigestion, etc.? It was also by design.

As the saber-toothed tiger draws closer to you, your body realizes this is not a good time to target and fight off bacteria, viruses, or any other microorganism that can cause disease. Remember, it needs to redirect all energy towards fighting or running! Therefore, your immune functioning will be lessened because it's not a priority. During your last major stress episode, did you find yourself getting sick during or soon after the episode (a cold, flu, sinus infection, allergy flare-up, etc.)? It was by design. Some people even go as far as turning on an autoimmune situation that they were never intended to have or worsening the state of one they were already were battling (i.e. having what is known as a "flare," like a lupus flare, eczema, or psoriasis flare, multiple sclerosis flare, etc.).

These were examples of systems that could be weakened, but what about the systems that get turned up to a level ten to quickly deal with the stressor/perceived threat? As the saber-toothed tiger draws closer to you, your body realizes the moment calls for a fight and/ or flee from the tiger, so it will redirect energy to prioritizing your muscular function, to enhancing your vision (dilation of pupils), to increasing your blood flow (increase of heart rate), to increasing your oxygen flow (increase of respiration rate), etc.. Imagine your last major stress episode. Did you experience any fatigue, racing heartbeat, maybe even palpitations, shortness of breath, etc.? It was all by design.

Here's the most important part: We were meant to encounter a tiger every now and then, deal with it, and debrief so that your body receives a signal that the stressor is now gone, and every system that was diminished can be elevated back to its fully-functioning capacity and every system that was maximized is reduced back to its normal functioning level. However, the high-stress society of today translates into us encountering multiple tigers a DAY. Whew! With this schedule, it is virtually impossible to fully and appropriately debrief after EVERY tiger encounter; there's just not enough time in the day for that. We either need to reduce our tiger encounter frequency or enhance our body's response to them by pouring more intention, energy, and time into our stress debriefing actions. Many of us have ignored the debriefing actions (or stress management actions) for so long that the systems diminished during the stress response have been diminished too long and now operate in this compromised degree. Eventually, we consider it our normal, or need medications to manage it, resulting in further diagnoses. The consequences of doing so are expensive and ongoing. Similarly, many of us have ignored the debriefing actions (or stress management actions) for so long that the systems going full throttle during the stress response have been going full throttle for so long that now they are operating in an unhealthily heightened degree, which we call our new normal, and the same consequences follow. Your body becomes fertile ground for chronic inflammation, which it was never designed to experience. Or it causes a worsening of conditions you already have, and possibly even premature death.

    This is why stress management is nothing to play with. The once a month or even once a week 30-minute yoga session is not enough to balance encountering so many tigers a day. A good compromise is finding an activity you can commit to each day, even for just 15 minutes, that allows for appropriate debriefing – disconnection from stressors mentally, physically, emotionally, and spiritually. It should allow for time with yourself to acknowledge the stressors (we do not "ignore" them), taking in what they are, how they make you feel, why they make you feel this way and have this much power over your physical being, etc. For this reason, journaling is an excellent debriefing activity. It gives you an opportunity to consider these things so you can devise healthy, practical solutions. What parts of you are resonating with this stressor that allows it to be in your life in this way or for you to be controlled or on the receiving end by its impact on you? What can you alter about your perspective? What can you elevate within your lifestyle to impact this stressor?

Meditation and conscious breathing exercises are two of my favorite debriefing activities. If you are interested in learning more about pulling in the powerful tool of manipulating your breath to reduce stress, I highly recommend both my eBook called "Your Breath Is Your Super Power: A Guide to Conscious Breathing" (available for download on my website, ElevateWithDrK.com), and guided "Conscious Breathing Session" (available on my "Elevate with Dr. K." YouTube Channel)!

Whatever you choose, be sure to do it daily. You decide when during the day is best to maintain consistent practice (either at the beginning of the day to set the tone for your day, in the middle for a quick restart, or at the end to debrief from the stressors of that day). The power is in your consistency. If you need to add in extra accountability, do it. Do whatever it takes to avoid becoming a victim of chronic stress.

REST

When it comes to resting, our perspectives must shift. Merriam-Webster defines rest as "a bodily state characterized by minimal functional and metabolic activities...freedom from activity or labor...a state of motionlessness or inactivity...peace of mind or spirit" (3). Reflect on rest through the lens of it being the root word in restoration! This is your body's time to restore, rejuvenate, refresh, and reset itself.

Furthermore, it is extremely important to draw the distinction here between resting and sleeping. When you are sleeping, you are resting; but when you are resting, you are not always sleeping. We all have heard at some point in our lives about the extreme importance of good quality sleep, yet rarely do we hear about the extreme importance of good quality REST.

It is for you to identify what it looks like for you to be resting yet awake. Then, begin applying that on a daily basis. A lot of the activities that fit the criteria can also double as a stress management activity, so you are killing two birds with one stone. The significance of rest cannot be overshadowed. If you do not pick a day to rest, your body will pick it for you, and the day your BODY selects may not be a favorable time for you. So, take the lead and make sure you are providing your physical realm with regular and adequate restoration time.

Oh, and let's not just gloss over the SLEEP portion of resting! Good quality sleep is a necessity for optimal cellular function and overall health. What do I mean by good quality? Well, not only hitting the recommended hours of sleep, but those hours should reflect sound, uninterrupted sleep. This high quality of sleep represents you successfully transitioning through each stage of the sleep cycle. Each stage holds its particular benefits and is essential for its own reasons. When you understand the relevance of what goes on in each stage, it's easier to understand why sleep experts make such a fuss over consistently obtaining good quality sleep that is in alignment with your body's natural circadian rhythm (in reference to what portion of your 24-hour day you devote to getting in your 7-9 hours of sleep). Please see the diagram below for an overview of the sleep cycle for better understanding.

THE STAGES OF SLEEP

STAGE 1 — Transition to sleep
- Transition between awake and sleeping
- Light sleep/easily woken
- Experience eye, body, & muscle movement
- Lasts about 5 minutes

In stage 2, more stable sleep occurs. Chemicals produced in the brain block the senses making it diffuclt to be woken.

STAGE 2 — Light sleep
- Most time spent sleeping in this stage
- Eye movement stops & heart rate slows
- Brain waves/activity level becomes slow
- Lasts about 10-20 minutes

Growth hormone is released during stage 3 and 4. Most Deep Sleep occurs during the first third of the night.

STAGE 3 — Deep sleep
- Difficult to be woken up
- Would feel cranky & disoriented if woken up in this stage
- Slow brain waves appear during this period

STAGE 4 — Intense deep sleep
- Deepest stage of sleep
- Essential stage for proper sleep
- Lasts about 30 minutes

STAGE 5 — REM or Dream stage
- Dreams occur
- Eye movement is fast
- Brain activity increases
- Heart rate & blood pressure increases
- Arm & leg muscles paralyzed

REM sleep revitilazes the memory. In this stage, brain activity is very high and intense dreaming is more likely to occur.

All these combine to make 1 sleep cycle which is about 90 minutes long on average but can be up to 120 minutes.

For most people, a good night's sleep is around 4-5 cycles long.

Good Quality sleep requires both non-REM & REM sleep in uninterrupted cycles.

Be intentional around enhancing your sleep hygiene. Seeking professional opinions around evaluation and management of more physiological occurrences that can interrupt your sleep quality (i.e. imbalanced hormones, sleep apnea, etc.). Also, prioritize your sleep time over other things that could be going on in your life and getting in the way of this pivotal pillar. The whole "I'll sleep when I'm dead" mentality is a great example of collective ignorance and embracing it will have you bringing that statement to fruition a lot sooner than was intended for you. Remember, as you are elevating your sleep quality, whether you are currently hitting the recommended 7-9 hours of sleep per day or not, you still owe yourself REST time that should be honored every 24-hour period.

PHYSICAL ACTIVITY

When it comes to physical activity, our perspectives must shift. When people think of enhancing this realm, they quickly run to their local gym to purchase a membership, but it's not the only means and may not be necessary. The focus here is MOVING more. Physiologically, we were designed to move. Consider for a moment the perspective that exercise is optional, but movement is essential.

We, as in HUMANITY, have been becoming more and more sedentary over the years and have been trying to mold this into a "new normal." In today's society, we prioritize convenience and accessibility over movement. Long gone are the days of hunting and gathering, which required us to move to capture prey (or avoid becoming prey ourselves). Now, you can wake up and travel to a job sitting comfortably in a vehicle, then spend about 8 hours sitting (usually) comfortably behind a desk, stop at a grocery store or sit in the vehicle while food is delivered to you, get home and sit on a couch until food is ready, and all without overly exerting yourself. Then, of course, we're back to bed to lie down for several more hours.

This may not be your life all the time, but more often than not we find ourselves falling into extreme stretches of inactivity and/or low exertion. This lifestyle most certainly contributes to whatever you are currently not happy with physically. Again, there is exercise and then there is movement. The big picture in this pillar of your lifestyle is not about killing yourself in a gym, knocking out reps of a routine while simultaneously feeling that what you are doing is a chore. If you are not enjoying the process, then you should re-evaluate it because it will not be sustainable long-term. Here lies the main difference between exercise and movement. Exercise is something that we established to fulfill the movement box of our lifestyles. Unfortunately, this box can create a false notion that we are sufficiently moving. Furthermore, as I stated above, for some people it is perceived as a chore or an activity done out of obligation. That only adds more stress, and we've discussed already why that's not conducive to your elevation.

Even if you are exercising and love it, make sure you are still MOVING outside of your workout sessions, consistently. If you are exercising and don't like it, make sure you are getting your heart rate up and sweating via an activity you find pleasure in for at least 30 minutes, at least three to four times a week. Movement can take many forms: dancing, skating, hiking, yoga, martial arts, swimming, etc. It doesn't always have to be hopping on a fancy machine or using complex equipment at a gym. Once you begin getting in your sessions of activity, make sure you are still MOVING outside of it regularly too. Never forget the following statement made by Ido Portal, "The body will become better at whatever you do, or don't do. You don't move? The body will make you better at NOT moving. If you move, your body will allow more movement." (4).

TOXIN EXPOSURE REDUCTION

When it comes to toxin exposure, our perspectives must shift. Recall from the section on diet that nutrients act as the driving force of your cellular processes; the dialect or language that the cells speak; the currency of communication exchange between organs and organ systems at large. When things make their way into your body, whether it be via inhalation, oral consumption, topical absorption, etc., whatever percentage that is not breaking down into a valuable nutrient may be getting tossed into the toxin category by your body. It is a foreign entity that your body is unsure about.

Many relate toxin exposure to things like air pollution, contaminated water, second-hand smoke, lead/heavy metals exposure, chemical-ridden toiletries, and cosmetics, etc., which are all true. However, I want you to consider that about half of the toxins sitting in your body right now are coming from a different source – your food! Yes, when you consume things like genetically modified foods, inorganic foods, highly processed foods, etc., so much of that food content is not breaking down and being absorbed as a valuable nutrient. In fact, when you pick up a can, jar, bottle, box, bag, etc., of something processed to eat and flip it to the back where the ingredients are listed, you usually see a list of ingredients you cannot even make sense of – they are either difficult to pronounce or look like chemical words. You have no idea what they are, and the interesting parallel is that your body has no idea what they are either. Therefore, it is easily perceived as a toxin.

When the body is overwhelmed with these unfamiliar substances, aka toxins, it has to find a place to store them. They must be moved out of the way. These toxins have no designated place to go within the body like nutrients do, so the body has to find it a new home. Oftentimes, they are stuffed into some of the body's least complicated cells, the fat cells. Over time, this can result in an increase of the size of your fat cells, which can manifest as weight gain. Herein lies the connection between toxins and weight management. When someone is interested in losing weight, for instance, one of the first things I ask them to tell me is the date of their last detox. Similarly, when I am trying to educate on restoring balance to the body, reducing chronic inflammation, and optimizing organ system functionality, one of the first things I ask for is the date of the last detox. Detoxing, or the removal of toxins, is extremely important because no matter how clean you eat and drink, no matter how purified your air is, no matter how natural your toiletries, cleaning products and cosmetics are, you will still always have toxins in your body to some degree. It is impossible to avoid them ALL on a daily basis. This is especially true for those who have not yet fully addressed the other areas of their lifestyle. The frequency of your detoxing is up to you, but it should be linked to the amount of toxins YOU introduce into your body. The person I just described with the clean eating and drinking, purified air, and natural toiletries, cleaning products and cosmetics will need to detox less than the person who consumes fast food and sodas, has no access to clean air and water, and is using chemical and heavy metal-ridden toiletries, cleaning products and cosmetics. Chances are, if you have not detoxed in the last 6-9 months, you probably need to. Let's start there.

A great detox does not have to include expensive and aggressive detox products, or consuming an unfavorably tasting drink concoction. A great detox simply needs to offer your body a means of reducing the toxin load it contains and replenishing the body of valuable nutrients it has been missing out on and/or that were stripped away during the detoxing process. A milder detoxification process does not lead to over-stripping (the loss of some good things in addition to the removal of the bad ones). The good stuff is simultaneously replenished while the body is cleansed on a cellular level.

I have created such a detox that involves a simple restructuring of how you eat for 21 days. It consists of three weeks of experiencing a highly anti-inflammatory way of eating. I have taken the common, Western diet and removed those food groups that cause an overproduction of mucous and chronic inflammation in the body (i.e. animal dairy products, animal meats, processed sugar, processed foods, etc.); and replaced it with a focus on incorporating nutrient-dense foods that serve our bodies more positively (i.e. whole foods, increased water intake, natural sweeteners, etc.). I call this my 21-Day Reset! In just 21 days, you can enact a powerful shift within your body – once the cells and organs are able to reset themselves, that's when the magic begins and you have access to experiencing things like chronic inflammation reduction – remedies such as blood pressure reduction, blood sugar reduction, blood cholesterol reduction, weight/inches reduction, pain reduction, enhancement of hormone metabolism, energy and immune system boosting, amplified cognitive functioning, and much more.

Please find my 21-Day Reset next page.

DR. K.'S 21-DAY RESET

ALLOWED DURING DETOX
- Fruits (try to aim more so for berries)
- Vegetables (try to aim moreso for cruciferous vegetables)
- Whole, Natural Grain Carbohydrates (inclusive of bread, pasta, rice, crackers, etc.)
- Nuts and Seeds (inclusive of nut butters, seed butters, nut milks, etc.)
- Legumes (inclusive of dried beans, pinto beans, split peas, lentils, black-eyed peas, kidney beans, black beans, cannellini beans, white beans, etc.)
- Healthy Fats/Oils (inclusive of olive oil, grapeseed oil, coconut oil, avocado oil, etc.)
- Beverages: Water and Herbal Teas Only
- Other: Vinegar (especially apple cider), Seasonings (especially more natural herbs, spices, Himalayan pink sea salt), Natural Sweeteners (especially raw organic honey).

NOT ALLOWED DURING DETOX
- All Animal-Sourced Meat (inclusive of beef, lamb, pork, seafood, poultry, etc.)
- All Animal-Sourced Dairy Products (inclusive of milk, cheese, cream, butter, eggs, etc.)
- Processed Sugar (inclusive of baked goods, candy, etc.)
- Artificial Sweeteners (inclusive of Splenda, Sweet and Low, Equal, etc.)

- Refined and Processed Foods (inclusive of starchy, white carbohydrates like rice, pasta, bread, potatoes, etc....also inclusive of frozen/TV dinners, fast food, excessive artificial colors and flavorings, food additives, chemicals, etc.)
- Deep Fried Foods (inclusive of chips, fries, breaded foods, etc.)
- Solid Fats (inclusive of shortening, margarine, butter, lard, foods high in fat, etc.)
- Beverages that are NOT water and herbal teas (inclusive of coffee, carbonated beverages/soda, energy drinks, fruit juices, etc.)

REMEMBER:

Read the labels on the back of every product you purchase! The first thing to look at is the ingredients list (especially paying attention to the first three to five items listed, as they are going to be the ingredients most heavily incorporated in the product. Ingredients are listed in order of quantity, with the first item being what the product is most comprised of). The second thing to look at is the section directly above the ingredients list, for the total number of grams of everything (especially sugar and sodium).

Maintain proper daily water hydration, as this will expedite your toxin elimination process and amplify your detox results! Remember, the goal is achieving consistency with the daily consumption of half your body weight in ounces (i.e. a 200-pound person would aim for about 100 ounces of water each day).

LEVEL 4

SPIRITUAL WELLNESS

"Many are out here winning materialistically, but at the terrifying expense of losing spiritually." –Dr. K.

THE NONPHYSICAL ASPECT OF A PERSON – THE SEAT OF EMOTIONS AND CHARACTER

As we begin our spiritual wellness journey, it is imperative that I highlight the distinction between spirituality and religion. Remember, this is SPIRITUAL wellness via your alignment with the spirit realm, not RELIGIOUS wellness via your alignment with a religion, a domination, doctrine, etc.

Religion usually entails adhering to a certain dogma or belief system (Christianity, Islam, Judaism, etc.), whereas spirituality places little importance on intellectual beliefs, but is more concerned with growing into and experiencing the divine consciousness and spirit of God. Your spiritual wellness is then your journey or quest for meaning and purpose in human existence, leading you to strive for a state of harmony with yourself, God, and others. Your spiritual wellness also incorporates the comprehension and application of elementary spiritual principles such as hope, faith, obedience, discipline, humility, balance, grounding, etc. Therefore, taking care of yourself holistically (each and every facet of your health and wellness), is an honorable spiritual act of the highest order! In fact, TRUE self-care launches you into the space of self-love – an exceptionally high vibrational frequency. Whether you are making tweaks to your diet, adding more movement sessions into your schedule, being intentional about speaking positive affirmations over yourself daily, etc., you will be exercising one or more of the fundamental spiritual realm principles discussed previously. Therefore, doing the work to become the very best version of yourself mentally, physically, and spiritually is one of the greatest acts of reverence and appreciation of God.

AVOID SPIRITUAL STAGNANCY!

When working to enhance your spiritual wellness, it may help to consider that the language of the spirit realm is vibration and the currency is energy. This is the importance of keeping your vibration as high as possible, as often as possible. Many feel that we are physical bodies with a spirit inside, when we in fact are spiritual entities possessing a physical body. When we communicate with one another on a spiritual level, this communication (vibrations) is received and understood loud and clear. Hence, the importance of aligning your vibrations (spirit realm) with your manifestation intentions (mental realm). If you are trying to manifest something, but your vibration is low (i.e. due to being consumed by fear, illness, negative thoughts, etc.) then it will be nearly impossible to make your intention a reality. Despite what you are saying, it is your vibration (the summation of your current alignment within all realms, and with that which you desire) that gives the final say so in the realization of your intention. For instance, if you are battling cancer, and you set the powerful intention to be whole and well, spirit realm will pick up on any stray thoughts or emotions around fear, anger, resentment, guilt, etc. that will throw off your alignment. Spirit realm will pick up on these frequencies. Your intention was stated powerfully, but your vibration was low, which will impact the overall power for manifesting.

Considering the currency of the spirit realm – energy – is another way to ensure that you are attracting what you wish to attract and manifesting what you wish to manifest. You need to understand and respect the fact that energy must flow. It is through this circulation that we receive blessings and abundance. Interruption of the flow, or spiritual stagnancy, is an easy way to block the reception of blessings and abundance. For instance, as mentioned earlier, if you are interested in attracting more money to yourself you need to give money through your discipline and obedience to the principles of gratitude, the total trusting of God and the total trusting of the process. This is how you keep the flow circulating. The notion that most people have of holding on to money because "I have so little and it would be crazy to give some away" is emitting a frequency of scarcity and fear, which is then (according to the Law of Attraction) what you will attract more of. However, giving money (i.e. tithing in church, donating to charities, giving to the homeless/needy, etc.) because "I have so little and want to align myself with GRATITUDE of the little I have, TRUST in the fact that more is to come, and GIVING to solidify my respect of the process" is emitting a frequency of abundance, allowing the circulation of money to flow back to you uninterruptedly. Thus, spiritual stagnancy is successfully avoided.

SPIRITUAL HYGIENE

It's important to apply the same intensity used to maintain your other realms (i.e. physical realm, mental realm, etc.) to your spiritual realm. For instance, parallel to the physical realm, you will need to engage in spiritual cleansing, detoxing, use of supplements, examining/assessing, etc. The occasional and inconsistent meditation or journal entry is the equivalent of you taking your Vitamin D supplement only every now and then, but then wondering why your test results indicate the same levels. Ask yourself now, what DAILY actions contribute towards your spiritual realm grounding and elevation? If your answer is "nothing," what ideas come to mind that you can begin to implement? If you are doing something already, but not daily, get present about what is in the way of you doing it more often and how you can address that so it is no longer an obstacle for your spiritual growth.

What are examples of things that you can do daily to encourage your spiritual growth? Well, I'm glad you asked! Anything that advances you closer to your creator, the Most High, God. This is inclusive of anything that will help you with discovery and alignment of the purpose assigned to you by God, your spiritual gifts provided to you by God, and your authentic and higher self created in the likeness of God. Following this broadens your options from just wearing healing stones, burning sage, and sitting for the occasional meditation to check the box of spiritual elevation. This allows you to pull in your creative mind to have these things enhance your connection, or to come up with entirely new practices all together. This calls on the important notion of DOING THE WORK. What work are you doing to maintain divine alignment in your life? Prayer is miraculously powerful, but what are you coupling with it to enhance its impact over your life? For instance, are you solely praying to become a better person and to have a better life; or, along with prayer, are you incorporating the WORK that you are doing to audit and enhance all aspects of yourself and your life? Are you going hard and being consistent with your spiritual hygiene even when things are going well, or do you only wait for chaos and imbalance to occur to then scramble to fulfill acts within the spiritual hygiene category?

This is the difference between those who read this book, find it wonderful as a leisure read, and go about their regularly scheduled program versus those who read this book, get convicted and inspired, and use the motivation to elicit practical application of the learnings within this book into their lives. You will visibly be able to see the difference between these two individuals, as the latter will begin to manifest a changed life and an elevated consciousness. He/she will also be more likely to flow in a space of satisfaction and gratitude, as he/she shifts into alignment with his/her purpose.

Alignment with your purpose is hands down one of the most beautiful experiences to have while in this physical, Earthly realm. However, the prerequisite to aligning with your purpose is knowing what it is. Remember, we are all uniquely created with an equally unique purpose. We were also created with all that would be needed to execute this purpose – we have all the tools within us already. What a nice set up, right? So, when you know you have a purpose but do not bother to discover what it is; or when you know what it is but do not bother to align with it; or when you are not executing it because you never knew (until now) that you even had one in the first place, you are quite literally robbing humanity of experiencing the unique purpose that only you have.

When it comes to purpose discovery, the most important thing to understand is the astounding phenomenon that your purpose IS you and that you ARE your purpose! The entire reason that you are here on this Earth is deeply entangled with who you authentically are, at your core. Therefore, to profoundly understand one's purpose is to profoundly understand one's self. Therefore, as you begin the journey down the path of purpose discovery, you must begin the journey of uncovering exactly who you are, why you do what you do, say the things you say, think the way you think, stand for what you stand for, surround yourself with certain energies, etc. Let's begin.

PURPOSE DISCOVERY: CORE VALUES

I like to begin with getting clear on those fundamental principles that contribute to who you are at your core, otherwise known as your core values. These are the ideals that are present with you at all times – things that you stand for, matters that you would even die for. These sit at the foundation of who you really are, influenced by your life path (i.e. the place you were born, the teachers you have had, the family you had around you, the cultural traditions you were raised within, your own understanding of basic life philosophies, etc.). It's important to identify your core values. For example, if one of your core values involves "taking the higher moral ground and considering the interest of everyone involved at all times," aligning with this value raises your consciousness and gets you a step closer to flowing in your divine truth and power.

Take a quick moment to grab a notebook or a sheet of paper to complete the following exercise. Get yourself settled, comfortable, and free of distractions. Then, go ahead and glance at the chart of example core values. Let your eyes dance from word to word, column to column.

Keep a steady pace and jot down the words that jump out at you. Do not overthink it, do not try to rationalize anything, do not try to pick ones that sound good, do not try to pick ones that you WISH were core values you hold. Simply note those that resonate with you and keep going. Don't break the pace.

Accomplishment	Collaboration	Creativity	Fairness
Abundance	Commitment	Credibility	Faith
Accountability	Communication	Decisiveness	Faithfulness
Accuracy	Community	Democracy	Family
Achievement	Compassion	Determination	Flair
Adventure	Competence	Discipline	Flexibility
Approval	Competition	Discovery	Forgiveness
Autonomy	Concern for others	Diversity	Freedom
Balance	Confidence	Education	Friendship
Beauty	Connection	Efficiency	Frugality
Challenge	Conservation	Environment	Fulfillment
Change	Content over form	Equality	Fun
Clarity	Cooperation	Excellence	Generosity
Cleanliness/orderliness	Coordination	Exploration	Genuineness

Once you finish, take some time to sit with your findings. Is there a value that you know for a fact you hold dear but did not see on the list and wish to add now? When your list is complete, it's time to fine-tune it. Comb through your list, whether you've listed five or fifteen, and continue your reflection until you have three solid core values. This process may take days or weeks of revisiting. Use meditation sessions or quiet, reflective times with yourself. Do not feel you need to rush it. When you have your three values, go ahead and rank them in order of priority, with number one being the most important. Then, again, take time to sit with your list. Research multiple definitions of the values, journal or reflect on how and why these three values resonate with you most. Find areas in your life that demonstrate why you are most drawn to these three core values. Meditate on your alignment with them. If these are the three things you stand for the most, how do your DAILY choices, actions, thoughts, emotions, etc. consistently line up with them? How can you take this daily alignment to the next level, and what are your next steps in doing so? Expedite the manifestation of your alignment with your core values by creating a Manifestation Map around each of the three values!

PURPOSE DISCOVERY: SPIRITUAL GIFTS

Many people feel that they either do not understand what spiritual gifts are, or that they do not possess one at all. Let me start by saying, you have one. Some people have more than one, but everyone has at least one. This is yet another ability or tool gifted to us, empowered by the spirit of God to execute our purpose more efficiently and with a higher impact on humanity.

When it comes to identifying them, understand that you reveal them via self-discovery, which involves the spirit that gave you the gift in the first place. I say this because I have seen so many quick online quizzes and assessments that claim to tell you exactly what your spiritual gifts are. I have taken a few of these out of curiosity. Although I enjoyed the interesting insights from the assessment results, I know that self-discovery without God will always come up short. Just like the core values, you do not want to rush this. Uncovering your spiritual gifts will come through mindfulness and spending time with God with this intention at the forefront of your mind.

Also important, understand the difference between a spiritual gift and a natural talent. Many people have a difficult time differentiating the two. To make it as simple as possible, consider that natural talents are PHYSICAL abilities to do special things, whereas spiritual gifts are SPIRITUAL abilities to do special things. For instance, some natural talents might be musical ability, a knack for carpentry, mechanical aptitude, artistic skills, etc. Natural talents are often the vehicle through which spiritual gifts are utilized. A good example of this would be a famous gospel singer with the spiritual gift of evangelism who expresses this gift through the vehicle of musical talent.

Just as you did for the core values exercise, take a quick moment to grab a notebook or a sheet of paper and complete a similar exercise to jump start your journey of spiritual gift discovery. Get yourself settled, comfortable, and free of distractions. Then, glance at the chart of spiritual gifts below. Let your eyes dance from word to word, column to column. Keep a steady pace and jot down the words that jump out at you. Do not overthink it, do not try to rationalize anything, do not try to pick ones that sound good, do not try to pick ones that sound good, do not try to pick ones that you WISH were gifts of yours. Simply note the one(s) that resonate with you and keep going. Don't break the pace.

THE SPIRITUAL GIFTS

Foundational Gifts	Serving Gifts	Speaking Gifts
Apostle	Giving	Teaching
Prophet	Administration/Leading	Exhortation
Healing	Mercy	Pastor-Teacher
Miracles	Faith	Evangelist
Tongues	Helping	* Word of Wisdom
Interpretation of Tounges	Hospitality	* Word of Knowledge
		* Discerning of spirits

Many also classify these gifts as foundational, temporary gifts.

When you finish, take time to sit with your findings. Is there a spiritual gift you feel you possess but did not see on the list that you wish to add now? With your completed list, it's time to fine-tune it. Whatever number of spiritual gifts you have listed in your notes, I want you to repeat the exercise again and again until you identify one or two spiritual gifts. This process may take days or weeks to revisit. Use meditation and prayer sessions in addition to quiet, reflective times with yourself. Do not feel that you need to rush it. Once you have narrowed your list, rank them (if there are two) in order of priority, with number one being the most important. As you confirm your list, you want to keep in mind that it is going to be aligned with your core values.

Then, again, take time to sit with your list. Research multiple definitions of the spiritual gift(s) you have selected. Journal or reflect on how and why the one(s) you picked resonate with you most. Find areas in your life that demonstrate why you are most drawn to these particular spiritual gift(s). Meditate on how you are exercising your gift(s) daily, and how you can take the sharpening of the gift(s) to the next level - what are the next steps to do so? This is extremely important because you must understand that your spiritual gifts do not usually come developed and ready to go. It often takes time for the gifts to mature and develop into their full effectiveness, and it is completely up to YOU to mature your gift – it is YOUR obligation! This is important because gifts which are not used or developed can apparently be lost. Finally, almost just as unfortunate as losing a gift due to lack of development is losing a gift due to MISUSE or MISMANAGEMENT of the spiritual gift. Expedite the manifestation of your alignment with your gifts and the strengthening of your spiritual gifts by creating a Manifestation Map around it/them!

PURPOSE DISCOVERY: PASSIONS

What are you passionate about? I am sure this is not the first time that you have been asked this question. You may have an answer ready to fire off, but how much time have you set aside to investigate how clear you are on what passion actually means? I invite you to consider the fact that your passion is that which will help you create the highest expression of your spiritual gift(s). The reason you feel the fiery way you feel when you are flowing in your passion is because you are flowing in what is meaningful to you and engaged in what is central to your self-identity (i.e. aligned with your core values). Examples of passions I have heard from others include making people feel whole/well, doing very creative work, having unlimited physical-world resources, feeling and looking great 100% of the time, having perfect friendships/relationships, always having fun, being a leader within a community, etc.

Just as you did for the spiritual gifts and core values exercises, take a quick moment to grab a notebook or a sheet of paper to complete a similar exercise to help jump start your journey of discovering your passion. Get yourself settled, comfortable, and free of distractions. Then, begin to list phrases that really light you up inside, things that you are extremely passionate about, things that you could see yourself doing just for the fulfillment received from doing it (no compensation involved).

When you have finished, take extra time to sit with your findings. Take your completed, and fine-tune it. Whatever number of passions you have listed in your notes, repeat the exercise until you are left with one or two things you are extremely passionate about. This process may take days or weeks of revisiting. Use meditation and prayer sessions in addition to quiet, reflective times with yourself. Do not feel that you need to rush it. Once you have narrowed your list, rank them in order of priority, with number one being the most important. As you confirm your list, keep in mind that your passion(s) will align with your core values and spiritual gifts.

Then, again, take time to sit with your list. Really get present with how your passion looks in action. How taking the actions makes you feel. Who would be impacted most by you taking this action? Journal or reflect on how and why the one(s) you picked resonate with you most. Find areas in your life that demonstrate why you are most drawn to the passion(s) you selected. Meditate on how you are exercising your passion(s) daily, and how you can take exercising your passion(s) to the next level - what are your next steps in doing so?

Once the passions have been discovered, you might be the type of individual who wishes to explore monetizing their passions. If so, you want to devote time to identifying who would benefit from (and pay for) this special thing that lights you up. Be realistic about whether this could blossom into a career path, and if so, what you would need to do to ensure it happens. Also, consider whether you would continue to enjoy the passion if it became a job/career, or would doing so cause you to lose interest because now it is "work" and no longer simply something you love to do. Finally, take note of who needs your passion in their life, and aim to have conversations with them and people like them to gain more clarity around how, where, and when you could serve them.

As you confirm your passions, keep in mind that they will be aligned with your spiritual gifts and your core values. Also, as you begin incorporating and living in your passions more regularly, expect the mutiny so that it does not throw you off when it happens. When you seek your passion, there will be parts of you that go into rebellion. Whether stemming from a fear of failure, success, visibility, vulnerability, etc. or other not-so-good thoughts could arise, urging you to stop doing what you love for whatever irrational reason you come up with. The discouraging words could come from yourself and/or from other people. Either way, if you let these voices win, your passion will remain out of your grasp. You will need to unlearn many years of conditioning – i.e. from parents, school, partners, colleagues, etc. – and reassure the mutinying parts that your ship is sailing in the right direction.

This will also call for you to continuously re-affirm that the world NEEDS your passion. So, decide right now that it is possible to find it. Use your spiritual wellness principles and practices to gain clarity and guidance around it discovering it. When you do discover it, be assured that it will always guide you in the right direction. You can also expedite your discovery of and alignment with your passion(s) by creating a Manifestation Map around it/them!

PURPOSE DISCOVERY: YOUR WHY

Let's talk about your WHY. Your reason for being here in this realm, on this Earth, in the way that you are appearing now (i.e. gender, race, personality traits, character, etc.). It's your unique and immeasurable mission contrived by the spirit of God. Discovering your purpose represents discovering the manner you are meant to impact the world in a way that completely fulfills, inspires, and gratifies you. Your purpose aligns with your core values, your spiritual gifts, your passions, and even your dreams. Your purpose, and your walk with the spirit of God to execute it, gives profound meaning to your existence.

The two most common questions I get after teaching and coaching around the importance of purpose-discovery are: "So, what IS my purpose?" and "How do I ensure that I'm really aligned with my purpose?" When it comes to confirming what you feel your purpose is, that is not something that I can do for you. I can help steer you down the right paths, but the most accurate confirmation of your purpose will come from the spirit that assigned it to you (God) and the entity that is entangled with your purpose, embodies your purpose, and IS your purpose (you)! So, naturally, part of your purpose discovery will have to involve you carving out intentional time to spend with God (meditation and prayer) and with yourself (mindfulness and inward reflections). Remember, your purpose is designed to impact the world at large, so if you feel you have landed on it, but it is only self-serving, then you have a little more work to do in the process.

When it comes to purpose alignment, realize that taking the steps towards purpose discovery (i.e. doing the exercises you just finished reading about) automatically begins to shift you into alignment. You doing the work consistently draws your core values and passions into your day-to-day choices and actions. You doing the work refines and reinforces your spiritual gifts. You doing the work to elevate yourself mentally, physically and spiritually. Even the act of you reading this book and APPLYING the learnings... they are all components of purpose alignment! So, naturally, if aligning with your purpose is aligning with yourself, because you are an ever-transforming being, that means that your purpose will be constantly shifting, expanding and blossoming. This represents the shifting, expanding, and blossoming of your own perspective and consciousness, which has you constantly seeing and learning something new about yourself and your purpose as you elevate to a frame of consciousness that is ready to receive the expanded awareness of your mission. In other words, your purpose itself is not changing, but perhaps when you were of your lower self you did not have the capacity to receive certain things about it yet. You will receive to the degree of your awakening, and as you awaken the more revelations you will have about yourself and your WHY. Hence the importance of always striving to elevate your consciousness at your own pace. Don't bother comparing your pace to others – there is no race to the higher levels of consciousness. The key is to consciously take charge of your own reality, doing the daily work to achieve genuine and absolute alignment with your higher self and thus your purpose. When you focus on this, you'll notice that everything will slowly start to make sense and come together to contribute towards the highest expression of yourself and of your unique, God-given purpose!

LEVEL 5

ELEVATION OF CONSCIOUSNESS

"Be so sincerely committed to your elevation that you are willing to say no without guilt and yes without fear." –Dr. K.

SOCIAL WHOLENESS

Now that you have been equipped with how to continue discovery of and alignment with why you are here, I know you are thinking, "I'm so excited and charged to blow through this... but what do I do next?" Well, I'm so glad you asked! Mental, physical, and spiritual balance is not the end of the consciousness spectrum. In fact, I'd argue that it is only the beginning! This high level of holistic balance is more of a prerequisite to higher ascension. It represents one-fourth of a broader consciousness I will refer to as the WHOLE SYSTEM.

Your expansion of consciousness as you plug into the whole system is going to be one of the most powerful tools in your toolbox for your continuous purpose alignment! It will help your day-to-day choices become less daunting as you gravitate towards things that support your alignment and stray away from those that may stagnate or sabotage your alignment. This flow comes from you pulling on your elevated consciousness to make decisions and take actions on your own versus based on what you are told to do, what you see others doing, etc. This flow comes from the fact that you are now creating life, rather than feeling it is just "happening to you".

You are gracefully moving closer to God and impacting humanity in a positive way while doing so, rather than "swimming upstream" and struggling through life. You not only respect, but you BECOME the process! You embody the process of an ever-increasing spiritual or energetic awareness of the meaning of your existence, your spiritual essence, and the conscious nature in all living things.

The first quadrant of the whole system is what I like to call SOCIAL WHOLENESS. Imagine getting yourself mentally, physically, and spiritually balanced alongside other like-minded individuals who too were getting themselves mentally, physically and spiritually balanced. We would essentially create a nirvana-like ecosystem comprised exclusively of holistically balanced people interacting with one another. To me, social wholeness represents human harmony – being able to relate, engage, and experience one another on a level that many can barely imagine.

There are two significant realizations within this blissful reality. The first realization lies within the notion that birds of a feather really DO flock together. You literally are the sum total of the people you hang around. The people in your circle are a representation of what you deserve and what you do not, your ambition and aspirations, or lack there-of. Be aware and cautious of the different types of energies you allow into your space. You should aim to surround yourself with people and energy that you yourself aspire to become like and exude consistently. Your circle should be as inspirational and motivational as possible. The energies around you should empower you along your life journey and assist in keeping your vibrations high.

As you elevate and expand your consciousness, you will find that you will not be able to tolerate certain things, situations, and people any longer. A gentle distance may begin to grow between you and others who were a part of your circle for years and it won't seem forced or negative. It will be more like when people say, "We just grew apart." Or, certain individuals in your circle may begin "showing you their true colors" in a way that, with your new lens, what you see does not support or align with your elevation.

You may find that a certain food group you once freely consumed for several years suddenly leaves a strange taste in your mouth, or does not sit well in your stomach or with your mind or spirit. You will try and try again, receiving the same outcome. Then you can make a choice that supports your alignment with elevation.

You may find that a certain relationship or job no longer serves you. Nothing has really changed behavior or routine-wise, but your tolerance has noticeably shifted. You can then make a choice that supports your alignment with elevation.

The second realization lies within the notion that you and I are more alike than we are different. The same goes for you and your neighbors, you and your coworkers, you and your doctor, you and the President of the country... you and every other human you ever come into contact with. Do not be fooled by the barriers and labels we have created for ourselves within society (i.e. race, gender, age, culture, religion, income status, etc.) that give the appearance of division. We are all spiritual beings having a physical, Earthly experience. One of the most profound realizations you can make regarding humanity and social wholeness is that fact that you, I, and all of humanity are actually REFLECTIONS of one another. This sentiment helps bring into perspective concepts like The Golden Rule (do unto others as you would have them do unto you), the thoughts you have about yourself and other people, the cessation of putting certain individuals on pedestals, etc. I am you and you are me. We are one.

ECONOMICAL WHOLENESS

The second quadrant of the Whole System is what I would call ECONOMICAL WHOLENESS. This quadrant speaks directly to your relationship with money and your overall financial freedom. This quadrant is especially key for those who have finished reading the mental realm section, have diligently applied the guidance on manifestation and attraction of becoming rich, and have seen little to no results. The underlying cause of your blockage could be found within this realm. For many, they want money but have never considered the integrity of their connection with it. Why should you be blessed abundantly with something you don't understand, or could misuse and risk lowering your vibration?

Let's do some perspective shifting. The pieces of green paper that many people nearly die over on a regular basis are just that. Pieces of green paper. What you are chasing is the value assigned to the pieces of green paper. You want the ability to make moves in your life without a lack of this holding you back (aka financial freedom). I want you to consider this value assigned to the pieces of green paper to be energy. When you look at money as energy, your perspective begins to shift during your evaluation of your relationship to it. I believe that it is of no coincidence that we also refer to money as "currency."

Now that we recognize money as energy, consider the first law of energy (thermodynamics) and apply it to money. The first law of thermodynamics (aka The Law of Conservation of Energy), states that energy can neither be created nor destroyed; energy can only be transferred or changed from one form to another. The most important part of the realization that money is energy is the recognition that this energy is never destroyed or created. It just flows. Therefore, when you are trying to attract and manifest money, you are not creating money that pops up in your reality; you are instead attracting and manifesting the shift of the energy current to flow in your direction. No matter what is going on in the world, no matter how chaotic it seems, currency is never destroyed. It may look this way (i.e. in the cases of recessions, stock market crashes, etc.) but what is actually happening is that the energy current is being shifted away from how we normally see and experience it. So, there is a false perception of deficit because someone always benefits from the new shift. How can you position yourself to be on the receiving end of a current shift? Well, one powerful way (as already discussed) would be by increasing your vibrational frequency, by moving consistently into a space of gratitude. Indeed, gratitude goes beyond finding things you are thankful for and expressing appreciation of them. This is only the start. Next, you move into the next phase of gratitude: trust. Being grateful for all that you have requires a heightened level of trust that those things you do NOT have but want are abundantly on the way. This includes money. You desire and put in work to powerfully manifest a current shift in your direction, while simultaneously being authentically grateful for the money that you DO have and trust fully that more is to come. So, when it is time to attract, how do you energetically demonstrate to God, the universe, and your subconscious mind that that you ARE authentically grateful and authentically trusting? What does that look like? Well, I'm glad you asked! If being in a space (perspective, thoughts, and emotions) of authentic gratitude and authentic trust looked like an action, that action would most likely be GIVING. Yes, the giving away of things (whether tangible objects like food or money, or intangible concepts like enlightenment or inspiration) relays a clear message that you are so grateful for what you have already been blessed with and so trusting that more is coming that you are willing to dip into your own supply of it and give some away. Doing so aligns you with the energy current, facilitating its uninterrupted flow by giving, and not promoting any blockages by holding on. This concept may be confusing. Some of you might think, "Wait! So, if I need more money, I should give some of the little I have away?" Yes, because your support and honor of the process enables the current flow to swing back around to you! This is why, within the Christian church, many people report an increase in income once they began consistently tithing, rather than holding on to their money because it was so little. This is where the trust comes in. Trust in God, trust in the process, trust in yourself, trust in the laws, trust in the current, etc. Gratitude without trust is inadequate; and elevation of your vibrational frequency without gratitude is inadequate.

ECOLOGICAL WHOLENESS

The third quadrant of the Whole System is what I would call ECOLOGICAL WHOLENESS. This quadrant speaks directly to your relationship with other living species with whom we share this planet. There are living beings with consciousness outside of the human race, including the Earth on which we reside, which is also a living being with consciousness.

There is a wonderful quote from Thich Nhat Hanh that I love so much where he says, "We are here to awaken from our illusion of separateness." We are all connected, plain and simple. The connection is not selective. We (as humans) are not only connected to one another, but we are also connected to the plants, the animals, the algae and other microorganisms, the Earth itself, etc. Thus, since we are all connected, we are also all influenced by one another's actions (obviously) and thoughts, energies, and vibrations as well. There have been countless studies demonstrating the impact of our thoughts and energy on animals, plants, herbs, and food.

Take a moment to reflect on how you express connectivity, respect, and gratitude to other living conscious beings, whether directly or indirectly. What is your stance on how animals are treated by us as a whole? What is your stance on environmental concerns and preservation of nature? What is your stance on deforestation? Do you litter? Do you speak words of light and love over the plants in your home or office space? Do you practice walking or just sitting in nature to foster grounding and gratitude? What can you add into your normal routine to enhance your ecological wholeness overall?

It's important to understand that to heal our home (Earth) is to heal ourselves (those who inhabit Earth); and to health ourselves (those who inhabit Earth) is to heal our home (Earth). So, the renewal of humanity is therefore an imperative element in the achievement of ecological wholeness.

CULTURAL/ANCESTRAL WHOLENESS

The fourth quadrant of the Whole System is what I like to call CULTURAL or ANCESTRAL WHOLENESS. This quadrant speaks directly to your relationship with your culture, and the culture of those in your lineage who came before you. It highlights your knowledge and action of ancestral awareness and acknowledgement. This is very important because there will be areas of your perspective (the foundation of your thoughts, emotions, actions and results), that will be better understood through your comprehension of this quadrant.

Go ahead and take a moment to reflect on how you currently identify yourself, culturally. How does this identity relate to how you view life, the other people in your reality, your core values, your character strengths and weaknesses, your music preferences, your attire preferences, your dialect, your food preferences, etc.? Now, let's dig a little deeper. Can you answer the same questions about your parents? Can you answer the same questions about your grandparents? In fact, can you speak to your ancestors by name (i.e. how many generations back can you go before you no longer know names)? How do you feel in general about your ancestors as a collective and/or as individuals? For instance, as a collective, are you ancestors historically known for something more negative (i.e. enslaving a group of people, murdering a group of people, etc.)? Are your ancestors, as individuals, known for something more negative (i.e. molestation within the family, theft within the family, etc.)? How does this make you feel? One of the most important tools for remembering who you are in order to reclaim your power is knowing where you come from. Your perspectives, character traits, core values, standards, self-esteem, etc. are largely shaped by what you inherited and experiences you had during childhood.

The past itself is gone; it no longer exists and cannot be relived. However, you take the learnings and messages tucked inside situations and apply them as tools for your own personal development. In fact, there is a famous West-African word known as "Sankofa," which denotes the fact that the past serves as a guide for planning the future because it is this wisdom in learning from the past which ensures a strong future. This also applies to learning from what those who came before you did or did not do. This can refer to those ancestors who came before you within your direct bloodline (i.e. members of your family tree), as well as those who came before you who are not in your direct lineage but are still a part of your ancestry (collective), like Harriett Tubman. You can learn from the mindset and choices of specific ancestors, and you can learn from the mindset and choices of your ancestral group (i.e. Germans during the Holocaust, Nigerians during the Biafra War, African-Americans during slavery, etc.).

It's important to look at the good, the bad, and the ugly when examining your culture and ancestors. Everything is an important piece of your personal growth and trauma healing, to prevent unfavorable patterns passed down from generation to generation including mindset (i.e. a way of eating that causes specific disease to run rampant in a family) and underlying causes of unresolved trauma (i.e. molestation, domestic violence, etc.). Don't forget to celebrate the good things as well, as these may be strengths that you want to incorporate more into your lifestyle, mindset and reality (i.e. the resiliency of the Jewish people who were made to experience the Holocaust, the determination of all Indigenous cultures to continue thriving and protecting their civilization, the power and fortitude of Africans to survive the Trans-Atlantic Slave Trade and subsequent decades of dehumanization).

This level of healing is critical because it's rarely even considered. The lack of consideration regarding one's past is dangerous because it leads to experiencing a false sense of completion. Some wonder why things are not exactly how they want them to be in their lives, and these lingering blockages could be the issue. This quadrant allows you to evaluate sources of trauma that may have nothing to do with you personally but are entangled in your DNA or your perception of your reality. In other words, your wound is probably not your "fault," but your healing is definitely YOUR responsibility! If you do not evaluate this realm, your authentic and holistic healing will be at a great disadvantage and may be more prolonged than it needed to be. What's worse is that if you never heal what hurt you, you will bleed on people who did not cut you.

On the other end of the spectrum, just knowing something as simple as the fact that you a descendant of majestic royalty will reshape your perspective and influence, your daily choices regarding how you allow people to treat you, what you tolerate within society, and goals you aspire to manifest. Something so simple can reshape your outlook on life and the results you are getting. Armed with this knowledge you may move with more clarity and intention, because you yourself will one day become an ancestor and the actions you are taking right now will leave an impact on those coming behind you. If negative and careless, be careful – karma can skip you and hit your children/the next generation. If positive, this is how you can single handedly be leaving a meaningful legacy for your children/the next generation and positively impact humanity as we speak!

LEVEL 6

DO NOT DISTURB: ELEVATION IN PROGESS!

*"You need to wake up from your autopilot mode.
You have to live deeply and with more awareness so that you
can be attentive to each moment." –Thich Nhat Hanh*

LET'S GET TO WORK!

Now that you have been fully equipped with enlightenment and inspiration, I'm sure you are fully charged and motivated to get started. The common thing to do next, is to question where to insert these action points into your life. How exactly do you fit "elevation of consciousness" into your schedule? Well, you should approach it in chunks (not all at once), undertaking each category repeatedly. There's a continuous self-audit that must occur, where you are checking on and evaluating the status of each realm day-by-day. You are going to have to audit your mental realm, your physical realm, your emotional realm, and your spiritual realm. Perhaps you can devote one week out of the month to each realm, and then each day hop into the boxes that make up these realms (i.e. in the mental realm, looking into your perspective, your creation abilities, what you have been attracting and what have been manifesting). The self-audit consists not only of checking the status of each, but also taking the next step to see what you can implement (or eliminate) to elevate that realm/category for that day or week.

You see, there's so much to evaluate and elevate about yourself, there really is no time to worry about what the next person is doing. There's no time to waste precious moments on trivial things that are not aligned with what you're manifesting for yourself, your lifestyle, and your purpose anyway. Performing these regular check-ins, category by category, THIS is true self-care! It's so much deeper and so much more complex than getting a mani-pedi or massage (both of which are great acts of self-care, by the way). Self-care does not and cannot end there; it's just the tip of the iceberg, as you can now see.

I'd like to share with you a suggestion on how to implement this level of self-care into your daily routine. Time management is key, because the time we have to get this done is the one variable we all have in common. We all have 24 hours in a day. However, what makes you different than perhaps the people you admire or idolize is how the 24 hours are utilized. I want you to take your 24-hour clock and divide it into three equal sections, each comprised of eight hours. Now, I suggest you devote one entire 8-hour section to rest. Yes, a third of your day will be assigned to one pillar of your lifestyle within the physical realm of your wellness. Keep in mind the distinction between resting and sleeping, so that you know that if you only SLEPT for six and a half hours, you still have an hour and a half remaining to REST.

Now, the second 8-hour section, I suggest you devote to something(s) you are doing for others. Something you do that contributes towards enhancing the life of someone else. For the majority of people, this will be your occupation. If you are a teacher, you are facilitating the enhancement of knowledge for others. If you are a financial advisor, you are facilitating the enhancement of wealth or financial freedom for others. If you are a nurse, you are facilitating the enhancement of health and disease prevention for others. If you feel that your work is not contributing towards enhancing the life of someone else the way you would like for it to, you are not alone. Maybe people are currently tethered to a job they are not passionate about and don't feel fulfilled by doing. These people seek to fill the void with volunteer or philanthropic work that better aligns with their passions and mission to enhance the lives of others.

Now, the third and final 8-hour section, I suggest you devote to things you are doing to enhance yourself (i.e. the full self-auditing mission). Yes, this is exactly where that can fit in. The enhancement of yourself by hopping into each of your wellness realms, seeing where they are and where they are not, and devising your next course of action to elevate each category. It's also important to realize that the three realms will not always present as uninterrupted chunks of eight in real life. Your reality may present like 6 hours of sleep, then 2 hours of self-audit, then 8 hours of work, then 2 hours of rest, etc. You one day may also have to borrow time against one section to add to another. The key is balancing things out by the end of the week. Balancing is highly important, because within the three 8-hour sections, once balance is consistently achieved, you can now work towards what I call the sweet spot.

The sweet spot, which some people in the world, including myself, have managed to attain, is a beautiful and magical position to experience. When you look at your three 8-hour sections, the sweet spot is reached when the things you are doing for others and the things you are doing for yourself begin to overlap or look similar. For instance, me writing this book as a gift to humanity is in turn part of me doing the work to elevate myself. As you are inspired and charged while reading, so was I while writing. It becomes such a beautiful reciprocity of fulfillment and elevation, and no longer "work" or another "task" for me to complete. It is simply me operating within the sweet spot.

NO TIME TO WASTE! – FINAL REFLECTIONS

Now that you are nearing the end of this read, I'm sure you have had made many physical and/or mental notes, had multiple epiphanies, and experienced some light-bulb moments. Hopefully, this includes having redefined TRUE health and wellness, and the meaning of TRUE self-care! It should be clearer now to see that this high level of self-care – inclusive of audits, intentional choices, and consciousness expansion – requires quite a bit of work and time. Not in a "busy-work" or "overwhelming" type of way, but more of a "you should be so occupied with tending to and cultivating your own grass that you don't even have the time or mind to contemplate if the grass being greener on the other side" type of way. This is why you should never compare yourself to another person – your life, your health, your wellness journey, your consciousness elevation journey, your purpose discovery journey, your destiny alignment journey are each uniquely your own!

What is for me is for me, and what is for you is for you. Respect and love your process for everything that it is and everything it is not, in every single moment. This is the quintessence of living a creative, balanced, and aligned life experience that you completely love. Because life is exactly that – a PROCESS that you EXPERIENCE.

Another huge take-away is to be crystal clear about some of the most important spiritual philosophies. These will enable you to execute your purpose and continuously elevate yourself holistically while positively impacting humanity - your sacrifice and your obedience. When it comes to sacrifice, what are you willing to give up to ensure you are authentically growing and transforming? What are you willing to remove from your space because it is too toxic or too insulting to your spirit? What are you willing to let die so that you can truly live?

In that same energy, when it comes to obedience, what will you do once you put this book down? Will it go on a bookshelf among other great reads as you return to the same life and reality you were in prior to reading it, or will you use this book as a message (or for many, a warning) to take immediate action on implementing your various learnings? Will you show up for yourself and take a stand for your own personal development and consciousness elevation? Will you get off the bench of your own life and get into the game? Once you begin, will you continue to do what you need to do, even when you don't want to do it?

Remember, with each section of this book that you implement within your life, if you run into any stagnation or break-downs, don't beat yourself up. Realignment is a necessary part of life and a special opportunity for a profound learning experience. It's a chance for you to discover something deeper about yourself and grow. Begin getting to the root cause of why what happened happened through the lens of reflection. Start to pan out and look for instances where you also behave in this way, view things in this way, experience this same sort of outcome, etc. You see, how you do anything is how you do everything!

For instance, if you are trying to work on the stress pillar of your lifestyle to enhance your physical realm by removing all of your stressors, and you experience frustration because you cannot remove them all (i.e. your job stresses you out, but you can't just quit your job right now), then instead of sitting in that frustration, (which is actually increasing your stress levels and bringing you back to square one) shift from trying to control everything externally to altering things INTERNALLY. Work on shifting your perspective about the situation, because we often cannot control a stressor itself but we can certainly control our response to it.

Next, you would look into other areas of your life where you are working harder and not smarter by forcing external change rather than just fostering internal transformation. Perhaps you are in a relationship where you have been experiencing negative emotions and exhaustion due to your attempts to change the other person rather than changing your own perspective and accepting them for who they are (everything that they are and everything that they are not). The majority of people spend well over 50% of their lives trying to change people and things that they cannot change. That is a lot of wasted TIME, and time is one of our most valuable gifts during our experience in this Earthly realm. Remember, all we really get are TIME and CHOICES, so please be extremely wise with both.

Keep in mind that the work you have done (or not done); the seeds you have planted (or not planted) are literally painting the portrait of your currently reality. After reading and APPLYING the principles within this book, there is no reason for not doing the work and planting flourishing seeds. If there is anything that you want(ed) that you did not achieve after doing so, it falls directly on you. You are in your own way. I can provide the knowledge, the road map and even the inspiration, but I cannot save you from you. So, every day you must make the conscious effort to get out of your own way and do the work. Even when things get a little overwhelming, you must still do the work. You may need to enlist the help of those in your immediate circle. In fact, know that you were never meant to walk this journey alone. Your purpose is so immense that you should need to call on the aid of God and others within humanity to connect with you and assist you. Never be afraid to ask for help! On the contrary, NOT asking for help is more of a sign of weakness than asking for it! It reveals a buried insecurity and toxic conversation with yourself that you are not worthy enough of having your own needs regarded and accommodated. This represents an imbalance within your self-confidence and self-pride that should be addressed. Confronting the imbalances is an exceptional opportunity for inward healing to occur!

Always be excited about life's random opportunities to learn, heal, and elevate! This gets you yet another step closer to reclaiming your power and walking in your truth, because the more you learn the more you learn that you have a lot more to learn.

Live life fearlessly and fill your reality with unconditional compassion and continuous laughter. The "fearlessly" part is so key, because one of our biggest fears of all is seeing ourselves; and that is exactly what this book has prompted you to do – see yourself. So be bold and fearless as you apply your learnings and flow through life! As you continue to journey in your authentic power and truth, please be sure to impact humanity by spreading light, love, and gratitude daily. Why listen to me? Because I AM you (*smile*).

ACKNOWLEDGEMENTS

I must first give complete acknowledgement, gratitude, and honor to my almighty God who has never left my side, stopped showering me with favor, grace, mercy, and infinite blessings. My protector, my healer, my friend, my light, my all. I know I am privileged to have a very profound and personal connection to God, full of bi-directional communication and the truly divine experience of God's presence on a regular basis. My eyes always fill with tears at the thought of reuniting with God at the end of my mission in this realm and hearing "Well done, my faithful servant." I live each day with the knowing that I am aligned with the purpose God bestowed upon me and elevating humanity as I have been clearly instructed to do.

As God is a very patient God, I could have gone lifetimes before "getting it." My purpose, my passions, my destiny, my work, my impact on humanity. God would have waited, but my spiritual team was a little less patient. I acknowledge them because it is through their haste to assist me with "getting it" that I quickly spiraled closer and closer to my purpose, thus closer and closer to God. I am so very thankful for the spirits that walk my path with me and the ones who paved the way for me – my gentle spirit guides, the beautiful angels that flow with me including my powerful father, Frank M. Igah, Sr., and the rest of my honorable and noble ancestors.

I must recognize and cherish those who assisted in my character development and the nurturing of my passions. To my Earthly family, I thank you beyond what words can express. It is through your beautiful souls that I find my grounding, my balance, my mental anchor, and my remembrance of who I am. My better half (Rashawn Phillips), my perfect princess (Genesis Phillips), my queen mother (Flora O. Igah), my extraordinary siblings and twin flames (Flora E. Igah, Roswitha O. Igah, Madonna O. Igah, Frances C. Igah and Frank M. Igah, Jr.) - you all are part of my core and inner-most circle. I love you.

To my bonus family through marriage, to my extended family in Nigeria and various other countries of the world, to the future children of my family soon to grace this Earth, and to the loyal, high quality friends that I now regard as family... I sincerely appreciate and value each of your unique roles in my life. I love you.

I would be remiss if I did not express gratitude to those who used their extensive knowledge and THEIR own spiritual gifts to help me get to where I am today – my mentors. Mentorship has absolutely been a priceless part of my own elevation because my mentors sharpened me mentally, emotionally, physically, and spiritually in ways that I could never have received in school curriculums, training programs, or books. Thank you, Maiysha Clairborne for introducing me to the magical world of Integrative Medicine as a mentor and holding space for my growth within it as a soul sister. Thank you, Winston Cardwell for cultivating and affirming my natural healing confidence, aptitude and power. Thank you, Bryan E. Crute for convicting and strengthening my personal relationship and experience with God through your powerful teachings of God's word and pastoring of God's people. Thank you,

Jonathan L. Harris for enriching my spiritual wellness, helping me to sharpen and cultivate my own spiritual gifts, and pushing me to align with my higher self on a regular basis.

I would like to take time to also acknowledge those who acted as accountability partners ensuring that this book made it to completion in a timely manner. Anthony Joiner and his incredible book coaching team; the encouraging energy of Kieasha Hill, and the gentle yet steadfast push of Ayisha Jefferson.

It is through my obedience to God and everyone listed above that this book was manifested. May each of you achieve unlimited success in your own endeavors, protection as you flow through your own life journeys, and the knowing that I am here for you just as you have been for me steeped in the purest expressions of gratitude, inspiration, and reciprocity. I love you all and pray for continued blessings and peace over each of your beautiful souls.

REFERENCES

1. Epigenetics – Dr. Bruce H. Lipton
   https://www.brucelipton.com/
2. Centers for Disease Control and Prevention.
   www.cdc.gov
3. Merriam-Webster Dictionary
   https://www.merriam-webster.com/
4. Amazing Ido Portal Quotes, Training Methods and Videos
   https://www.fearlessmotivation.com/2016/04/20/ido-portal-quotes/

www.ingramcontent.com/pod-product-compliance
Lightning Source LLC
Chambersburg PA
CBHW050655160426
43194CB00010B/1949